C000282950

READING WITH THE ṚṢI

Studies in Comparative Literature
Jadavpur University

Studies in Comparative Literature, Jadavpur University is founded on the view that the study of literatures and the arts in multilingual and culturally diverse contexts such as India demands a comparative approach. It is informed by an interdisciplinary and intercultural focus on *bhasha* literatures, translation, orality and performance as well as other arts and digital humanities, in the context of local, national and international literary and cultural transactions. The series is meant for students, scholars and teachers of comparative literature as well as of single literature and other humanities departments. It brings together the work of faculty members and scholars at the Department of Comparative Literature, Jadavpur University, as well as of national and international visiting scholars who have enriched its research and debates.

Sub-series I: Texts, Contexts, Methods

Ia. Histories and Paradigms
Ib. Approaching New Challenges, Recasting Paradigms

Sub-series II: Indian and Asian Contexts

Sub-series III: Literature and Other Knowledge Systems

IIIa. Literary Studies and Performance
IIIb. Literature and Indigenous Knowledge Systems

Sub-series IV: Lecture Series

Contributions based on talks by Visiting Scholars

Series Editors

Kavita Panjabi, Professor, Department of Comparative Literature, Jadavpur University, Kolkata

Samantak Das, Professor, Department of Comparative Literature, Jadavpur University, Kolkata

Sucheta Bhattacharya, Professor, Department of Comparative Literature, Jadavpur University, Kolkata

STUDIES IN COMPARATIVE LITERATURE
JADAVPUR UNIVERSITY

SUB-SERIES IV: LECTURES

Reading With the Ṛṣi

A Cross-Cultural and Comparative Literary Approach to Vālmīki's *Rāmāyaṇa*

Robert P. Goldman

William and Catherine Magistretti Distinguished Professor of Sanskrit
The University of California at Berkeley (USA)

Orient BlackSwan

All rights reserved. No part of this book may be modified, reproduced or utilised in any form, or by any means, electronic or mechanical, including photocopying, recording or by any information storage and retrieval system, in any form of binding or cover other than in which it is published, without permission in writing from the publisher.

READING WITH THE ṚṢI

ORIENT BLACKSWAN PRIVATE LIMITED

Registered Office
3-6-752 Himayatnagar, Hyderabad 500 029, Telangana, India
E-mail: centraloffice@orientblackswan.com

Other Offices
Bengaluru, Chennai, Guwahati, Hyderabad, Kolkata,
Mumbai, New Delhi, Noida, Patna, Visakhapatnam

© Orient Blackswan Private Limited 2023
First published 2023

© for essay rests with author
© for General Introduction rests with Series Editors

ISBN 978-93-5442-282-9

036790

Typeset in Adobe Garamond Pro 12.5/15.6 *by*
Shine Graphics, Delhi 110 094

Printed at
Thomson Press, New Delhi 110 020

Published by
Orient Blackswan Private Limited
3-6-752, Himayatnagar, Hyderabad 500 029, Telangana, India
E-mail: info@orientblackswan.com

Contents

General Introduction

The first full-fledged department of Comparative Literature in India, and the second in Asia, was established in Calcutta at Jadavpur University in 1956. The reputed Bangla poet, writer and scholar Buddhadeva Bose was its founder and the first Head of the Department. The *Jadavpur Journal of Comparative Literature*, launched here in 1961, is one of the oldest journals in Asia that has continued, regularly, to publish significant research in comparative literature by national and international scholars. In the late 1980s the UGC earmarked the department for promotion of teaching and research under its Special Assistance Programme. In the early nineties the department widened its areas of interest to first introduce courses in the literatures and cultures of Bangladesh, Africa, Canada and Latin America; then it set up centres in the latter three, subsequently a Centre for Translation of Indian Literatures, and, most recently, a Centre for Studies of Islamicate Asia. During the Tenth Plan the department was also selected by the UGC to participate in its ASIHSS (Assistance for Strengthening of Infrastructure for Humanities and Social Sciences) programme. In addition to these UGC programmes and these centres, the UPE—University with Potential for Excellence—programme of the UGC also enabled the establishment of research projects in the department. These included translation and intercultural studies under Project Anuvad; documentation and research relating to performers of traditional dramatic forms in different districts of West Bengal under Project Palagaan; and a unique new venture involving an exploration of Kolkata through narratives of sound under the project Soundscapes. The first and so far only UGC Centre of Advanced Study in Comparative Literature in India was also established in this department in 2005, and it continued promoting research into its third phase. This series, Studies in Comparative Literature, Jadavpur University, is rooted in this academic history of over six decades.

When other departments of Comparative Literature finally began to be established in India in the 1990s, a sharing of our research and pedagogic experience became imperative. As the practice of comparative literature proliferated in centres and newly established departments as well as in single literature departments right across India, we began to face persistent requests for enhanced access to our research from academics, researchers and students alike. Our research, while considerable, had largely been published by local presses and the university, and did not have the national outreach now demanded of it. It was in response to this need that the idea of initiating a series with a reputed mainstream national publisher came about, and we are especially happy about this partnership with Orient BlackSwan, given the important role it has played in the dissemination of scholarship on Indian literatures and cultures.

We hold that the study of literatures and the arts in multilingual and culturally diverse countries such as ours demands a comparative approach; hence, Studies in Comparative Literature, Jadavpur University, is a series for students, scholars and teachers of comparative literature as well as of single literature, arts and other humanities departments. It explores a range of histories, theoretical reflections, as well as innovative approaches and concerns relevant to the field of comparative literature. In keeping with the basic imperatives of comparative literature, it is both intercultural and interdisciplinary in that it engages with the trajectories of literatures across cultures as well as with the relations between literatures and other fields of creative expression. It is thus informed by an interdisciplinary and intercultural focus on *bhasha* literatures, translation, orality and performance as well as other arts and digital humanities, in the context of local, national and international literary and cultural transactions, and also those of the borderlands.

This series brings together the work of faculty and scholars at the department of Comparative Literature, Jadavpur University, and of national and international visiting scholars. It comprises both edited volumes and authored books, as well as monographs by visiting scholars. The series launches the research carried out under the third phase of the UGC Centre of Advanced Study in Comparative Literature, and the publication of these volumes, we hope, will mark the beginnings of a renewed mapping of comparative literary studies in India.

The current studies build on the foundations of creative intellectual vision, innovative pedagogy and several decades of original scholarship that went into the shaping of what was a new field of study, in fact a new mode of inquiry, in the Indian university. Many generations have enriched comparative literary studies in India, and it is impossible to chart all the contributions of even just those at the Department of Comparative Literature at Jadavpur University in the space of a short introduction such as this. What follows however is a brief account of the directions of research, and of the kinds of publications that emerged from this research, as well as in response to pedagogic needs at this department; it is being presented here as an academic contextualization for the present series that may be useful to other scholars, centres and departments of not just comparative literature but also literary studies in general.

Before mapping the broad areas of research across the decades however, it may be relevant to reflect for a moment on the intellectual and creative range of teachers and scholars who contributed to its making. Buddhadeva Bose and Sudhindranath Dutta were towering modern Bangla poets and writers, and amongst the foremost intellectuals of their time. Joining them in the early years were Fr. Robert Antoine, a Belgian Jesuit priest who was a Sanskritist and a scholar of Greek and Latin, who translated Kalidasa's *Raghuvamsa* from the Sanskrit into English, and also collaborated on a translation of Virgil's *Aeneid* from the Latin into Bangla; Fr. Pierre Fallon, who was also a Belgian Jesuit priest, a professor of French literature, a licenciate in philosophy and theology and an expert in Bangla philology; and David J. McCutchion who had trained in French and German at Jesus College Cambridge, and later became an authority on both the terracotta temples as well as the *patua*s (scroll painters) of Bengal. The next two generations of teacher-scholars, five of whom also trained in M.A. or Ph.D. programmes of North American departments of Comparative Literature and others in France or Germany, included Naresh Guha, Amiya Dev, Deepak Mazumdar, Subir Roychowdhury, Swapan Mazumdar, Bijoya Das, Subha Chakraborty Dasgupta, Ipsita Chanda, Suman Ghosh, Alokeranjan Dasgupta, Pranabendu Dasgupta, Manabendra Bandyopadhyay, Nabaneeta Dev Sen, Sibaji Bandyopadhyayand Debiprasad Bhattacharya. All of them earned international repute as scholars, and while the last was a polyglot and a renowned Sanskritist, the penultimate five were also major creative writers in Bangla.

It is perhaps the wide range of exposure and training, which was as rigorous as it may seem eclectic, that cautioned scholars of this department about strait-jacketing comparative literary studies into any definitive 'school' or methodology, or of limiting Indian literary studies within the political borders of the Indian nation state. So, even in their pioneering role, they refrained from formulating a Jadavpur 'school' of Comparative Literature, or privileging any comparative methodology over others. They also desisted from confining literary studies to inter-Indian literary relations only, and conscientiously trained their lenses on the wider South-Asian and Asian, Perso-Arabic and Anglo-European fields too; and eventually they reached out to Latin America, Africa and Australia, especially in relation to transactions with Indian literatures and cultures, but also otherwise. Such catholicity, in both approach and range, would naturally give rise to questions of delimitation and focus—and what emerges clearly as a connecting thread across the decades is that, in terms of both literary-cultural focus and methodological approach, scholars here responded to the ground realities and the needs of their times.

It was in the early 1990s that the consolidated programme of publishing started, supported by the Special Assistance Programme of the UGC; the focus in this decade was clearly on creating resources for research. Bibliographies of reception—of World Literature in Bangla periodicals, and of Bangla literature in South Indian languages—formed one thrust area. Translation became a focal point from the beginning: translation of material such as literary manifestoes in Indian languages, and discussions regarding the aesthetics as well as comparative literature methodologies of translation featured in this phase. Literary historiography in India featured as an important concern as did East–West literary interactions of the colonial period. The fourth area of concern was in relation to third-world contexts—to cultures of silence as well as the challenge of envisioning their futures—and this included reflection on African and Latin American literatures and cultures.

The focus on generating resources for comparative research continued through the next five years with translations across several genres (poetry, short stories, plays and excerpts of autobiographies) and several languages (that is, from Bangla into other languages such as Asamiya and English, and from Odia, Gujarati, Marathi and other Indian languages into English as well as Bangla). Also, the first phase had documented debates on comparative literary approaches to historiography; this one brought into focus issues of genology from a comparative perspective, with a volume tracing the *charit* as a genre. A third area of engagement was that of linguistic and cultural formations of self-identity across the literatures of Bengal and Bangladesh, thus bringing the literature of Bangladesh into the purview of our research. This phase was also marked by the publication of three volumes under the rubric of Literary Studies in India: on Literary Historiography, Thematology and Genology; it brought together reflections of comparative literature academics as well as scholars from other literature and humanities departments, on approaches to literary studies in India at the beginning of the twenty-first century.

In the first phase of the Centre of Advanced Study (2005–2010), we continued, on the one hand with the task of generating resources for research, such as the annotated bibliography of Bangla and Asamiya histories of literature;

on the other hand we extended the work on historiography to specific areas of study such as Indian English literature. Two new sets of concerns came into focus in this period. One set related to the need to document and study the fast-disappearing body of folk performances—the outcomes included the recordings and studies of *Manasamangal pala* and *Banabibir pala*. The other set of concerns was underlined by the realisation that most of our international focus had been on literary relations with the Anglo-European world, while those with other Asian cultures had not received the attention they deserved; thus the imperative to retrieve and explore these resulted in a focus on travel literature from Asia with focus on the collection of literary material along sea and trade routes, and the publication of a bibliography of travelogues to Asian countries in Bangla as well as an anthology of Bangla and Odia writings on colonial Burma. During this phase the additional support from the Assistance for Strengthening of Infrastructure for Humanities and Social Sciences (ASIHSS) programme of the UGC enabled research in South Asian contexts and resulted in the publication of a South Asian nationalisms reader, as well as a volume on the poetics and politics of Sufism and Bhakti in South Asia.

The following years, in the second phase of the CAS, were marked by more extensive and deeper research in the fields already marked out. At least three areas that had clearly emerged as thrust areas were:

- Comparative Literature: Explorations in Discipline and Methodology
- Roots and Routes: Intra-Indian and Intra-Asian Linguistic, Literary and Cultural Relations
- Literature and Other Knowledge Systems

Resources generated for research during this period included a handbook on terms and concepts in comparative literature, a volume on comparative literature in Germany, and textbooks on Indian Nepali literature in English and Bangla. The publications on comparative explorations in genre included a study of the *namah*. Research on folk cultures as knowledge systems resulted in publications on *charak* and *gajan* in Bengal, another on Karbi oral traditions in the Northeast, as well as a volume on literatures and oratures as knowledge systems, based on texts from Northeast India. A comparative study on the *ghumantoo* roadies, or wanderers, of India and Canada added to this set. In the context of Asian studies, research was published on tales of medieval China. The research on South Asia extended itself to comparative studies of the literatures and cultures of borders in South Asia and the Americas; this last volume marked entry into a new area of research—Comparative Border Studies.

The present series has been envisioned as follows:

Studies in Comparative Literature, Jadavpur University

Sub-series I: Texts, Contexts, Methods

1a. Histories and Paradigms
1b. Approaching New Challenges, Recasting Paradigms

Sub-series II: Indian and Asian Contexts

Sub-series III: Literature and Other Knowledge Systems

IIIa. Literary Studies and Performance
IIIb. Literature and Indigenous Knowledge Systems

Sub-series IV: Lecture Series

Contributions based on talks by Visiting Scholars

In many ways it marks a deepening and consolidation of perspectives across the earlier decades of research; in other ways it also charts new directions in comparative literary studies. The sub-series **Texts, Contexts, Methods** includes two histories in the section *Histories and Paradigms*—one of the emergence and establishment of Indian Comparative Literature, the other a disciplinary and institutional history of comparative literature in India, based on documents preserved at Jadavpur as well as gathered from across the country. Planned along with these are anthologies on texts, contexts and concepts, and on comparative literary studies in India, with contributions from scholars across the country. The section *Approaching New Challenges, Recasting Paradigms* will introduce research in new directions that responds to contemporary challenges. Comparative Literature as a discipline has historically crossed borders in terms of time and space. One of these volumes is a response to the now pervasive trans-national histories of migrants and refugees and, focussing on the Indo-Bangladesh border, it marks a shift from the prism of the 'national' to the prism of borders and frontiers, to the epistemological perspectives of 'borderlanders'; another volume charts the transformations in comparative literary studies in light of the mutual interactions between digital humanities and literary mapping in South Asia.

The sub-series **Indian and Asian Contexts** includes both intra-Indian literary translations and a mapping of linguistic, literary and cultural relations grouped under the rubric of *Roots and Routes*, as well as translations from Bangla and Urdu of fictional and discursive writings of Muslim literati in Bengal from the early twentieth century onward. Included in this sub-series are comparative studies of 'progressive' literatures, South Asian studies of transnational writers such as Ismat Chughtai, and studies of intra-Asian engagements such as Bengal's encounters with Japan in the twentieth century.

The third sub-series, **Literature and Other Knowledge Systems**, includes a volume on reflections on methodology in the translation of performance texts in the sub-section *Literary Studies and Performance*; the sub-section on *Literature and Indigenous Knowledge Systems* carries a comparative study of Karbi and Chakma narrative traditions of Northeast India, as well as another of creation songs from India, Canada, Australia and Southeast Asia.

Finally, the **Lecture Series** comprises volumes based on talks delivered by national and international visiting scholars who have enriched the research and debates of our department, and often taken us in new directions too. We are truly grateful to Alessandro Portelli, Professor Emeritus, University of Rome La Sapienza, and Tridip Suhrud, Professor and Provost, CEPT University, Ahmedabad, for their contributions on oral history and Gandhi's languages respectively, and for their generosity in permitting us to include earlier landmark essays in their volumes. We also extend our gratitude to Robert P Goldman, Professor, University of California at Berkeley, and Daniel Rycroft, Associate Professor at the University of East Anglia for having agreed to write for us on the Valmiki *Ramayana* and the humanities in India, respectively. We thank other scholars, who have collaborated in the research on some of our publications; they include Jatin Nayak, former Professor of Utkal University, Indranil Acharya, Professor at Vidyasagar University, Subha Chakraborty Dasgupta former Professor in our own department, Shraddhanjali Tamang, also a faculty member at Jadavpur University, and writer Manoranjan Byapari.

This series is the collaborative effort of all the faculty members of the Comparative Literature department: Suchorita Chattopadhyay, Kunal Chattopadhyay, Aveek Majumder, Sayantan Dasgupta, Sujit Kumar Mandal, Parthasarathi Bhaumik, Epsita Halder, Debashree Dattaray and Sumit Kumar Barua. They have been working concertedly towards its publication over the last several years; and while the individual volumes will carry their respective names as authors, editors and co-authors, it needs to be put on record that this series is finally seeing the light of day through one of the most devastating pandemics in history only because of their determined collective commitment and mutual intellectual inspiration. We are also grateful to our research fellows—who will be acknowledged individually in the respective volumes—for their selfless and cheerful support. Last but not least we extend our deep gratitude to Padmaja Anant of Orient BlackSwan for her patient wisdom and infinite patience—it has indeed been a pleasure working with her.

Kavita Panjabi
Samantak Das
Sucheta Bhattacharya
Series Editors

The first volumes of this series are being sent to the press with a heavy heart, for Samantak Das is with us no more. May the infallible spirit with which he contributed to the making of this series continue to enrich it in the years to come.

Reading With the Ṛṣi: A Cross-Cultural and Comparative Literary Approach to Vālmīki's *Rāmāyaṇa*

'La naissance du lecteur doit se payer de la mort de l'auteur.'
Roland Barthes[1]

How should we, as readers, in 2021 position ourselves in attempting to understand and interpret a literary work of the first millennium BCE? What are the elements in the text itself and its receptive history that can condition our efforts to grasp its meaning or meanings? Then, too, what are the factors in our personal or cultural identities, our *saṃskāra*s, if you will, that might colour or influence our reading?

Now, of course such questions must pertain to anyone's reading of any literary text, and we must always keep in mind the Sanskrit maxim, *bhinnarucir janaḥ*, that is to say, 'people have different tastes'. But a work such as the *Valmīki Rāmāyaṇa* presents a particular set of challenges to different kinds of modern readers. For one thing, there is its antiquity. It is, like its closely related text, the *Mahābhārata*, the product of an ancient civilisation. Thus, it is set in a social, political and religious milieu quite different from those of modernity even within the cultures of which and for which it was a product. It is filled with ritual, cultural and mythological references and indeed with terms for realia many of which had become obscure even by medieval times. The poem's language itself presents difficulties for the modern reader. It is composed in a slight variant of classical literary Sanskrit known as *ārṣa*, the language of the *ṛṣis*, or seers. Sanskrit, of course, is a famously rather difficult and learned language and, so, modern readers of the work—even those who speak modern Indian languages—overwhelmingly read it in translation.

Moreover, the immense influence of the *Rāmāyaṇa* across the many centuries that separate its author or authors from us, along with the work's unparalleled popularity and influence throughout the diverse nations and cultures of South and Southeast Asia, have led to its being re-envisioned in virtually all of the languages of that vast region in many of its religious cultures and media, from temple friezes to paintings, folk plays, dance and modern cinema and television productions. A result of all of this is that, while relatively few people in India and Southeast Asia have direct access to or even interest in Vālmīki's poem, many are familiar—even deeply so—with one or more influential regional *Rāmāyaṇa*s many of which are significantly different from the ancient epic poem. But that poem, in its own variant recensions and sub-recensions, is the oldest surviving version of the tale of the epic hero, Rāma, and, it would seem, the version that is the direct or indirect inspiration of all others.

So much, initially, for the work itself. Now let me turn briefly to the situation of the reader by asking her or him a few simple questions. First, dear reader, what is your ethnic, national or religious background? Did you grow up in a family, a community or a nation in which the Rāma story is widely known? If so, what version in what language are you familiar with? The late poet and folklorist A.K. Ramanujan famously wrote, 'In India and in Southeast Asia, no one ever reads the *Ramayana* or the *Mahabharata* for the first time' (Ramanujan 1991, 46). So, if your answers to these questions about your background are positive, then you will bring to a reading of Vālmīki many of your own, your family's or your community's understanding of the version or versions of the Rāma story that they know and perhaps love. Would you not compare Vālmīki's work, perhaps unfavourably, to the version you learned at home from a relative, a religious storyteller, a Rāmlīlā or a TV serialisation?

For hundreds of millions of Hindus worldwide, Vālmīki's poem is regarded as one of the principal works of Vaiṣṇava scripture even if particular communities among them know and cherish their regional versions of the story above all others. For Rāma, revered by Hindus as the seventh of the standard set of ten avatāras, or incarnations, of the Supreme Lord Viṣṇu, is among the most widely worshiped of all Hindu divinities and, as will be discussed below, has become a major icon of Hindu nationalism in contemporary India. Even though other versions of the tale of this towering figure have in many ways and in many different regions and communities come to overshadow the one first composed by the legendary poet-seer Vālmīki, his reputation is such that the conventional date of his birth is today the 'restricted' or optional Indian holiday Valmiki Jayanti (also known as Pargat Divas), and there is at least one temple dedicated to him. Beyond the Hindu fold, the Rāma story has long been told in various versions by Indian Jain and Buddhist authors while in Southeast Asia there are numerous versions of the epic tale in virtually all of the languages and cultures of both the Buddhist and Islamic countries of that populous region.

Then again, what if you, as a person of European or East Asian heritage, have no knowledge of a South or Southeast Asian culture and had never before encountered or even heard of any version of the *Rāmāyana*? Might you not then judge the work—either favourably or otherwise—against, for example, the ancient Greek epics or other 'national' epics that you might have learned in childhood or in school or university?

Religious, ethnic or national origin aside, how might such factors as gender, political beliefs and social milieux influence your judgement and appreciation of Vālmīki's monumental work? In India, from antiquity itself but, of course, much more so in modern times and in the west, the poem has been abundantly—even fulsomely—praised for its beauty, its religious sentiments and its ethical teachings. It has also been sharply critiqued by later poets, feminists, Dalit communities, regional political movements, Marxists, secularists, rationalists and progressives in general because of its representation and treatment of women, lower caste groups and Dravidian communities (Goldman 2019).

In this context and given the long and complex literary life and receptive history of the Rāmakathā, the tale of Rāma, reading Vālmīki's influential version of the story today is beset with complications. There is, moreover, yet another fundamental schism in the ways in which the work like others of its type has been and continues to be read. These may be summarised by using the anthropological or ethnographic terms, *emic* and *etic* introduced by the linguist Kenneth Pike (Pike 1967). The former term refers to the view and analysis of cultural or religious phenomena from inside the group within which they are practised, a sort of 'subjective' view, while the latter is used of analyses of such things from observers outside the target group, what has been called an 'objective' view. Both kinds of views, it hardly need be stated, are heavily conditioned by the personal, cultural and intellectual positionality of the observer.

In the case of the *Rāmāyaṇa*, emic readings go back into antiquity in the form of variants of Vālmīki's story found in Buddhist Jātakas, Jain Rāmāyaṇas, Vaiṣṇava Purāṇas, literary versions produced by Sanskrit and vernacular poets and dramatists, and the numerous Sanskrit commentaries the original work has engendered. This tradition is kept alive today by religious teachers, storytellers (Rāmāyaṇī-s), performing artists, filmmakers, to mention but a few.

Etic readings,which basically consist of scholarly studies of the *Rāmāyaṇa* produced by academics—philologists, literary scholars, historians, anthropologists, scholars of Religious Studies and so on, in India and worldwide, began to be written during the so-called Oriental Renaissance in eighteenth-century Europe (Schwab 1984). One may add translations of the epic in many languages to this list, beginning with Carey and Marshman's 1806–1810 Latin version, as opposed to the kinds of reworkings and re-envisionings mentioned above. True translations, no matter how literal or 'accurate' their translators strive to be, are necessarily products of innumerable acts of interpretation. For example, the many Jain versions of the Rāma story, although they are the products of such authors as Vimalasūri, who are very much products of their own times and cultures, read Vālmīki's work from what must be seen as their own etic point of view as their religious tradition and philosophy thoroughly undercut the Vaiṣṇava framing of their original. Then, too, modern Indian translations of the poem into English, works such as the Gita Press translation (1969 and 1998) and that of Hari Prasad Shastri (1952–1959), though they are standard, modern, more or less word for word translations, depend heavily at difficult passages on a widely published early modern and deeply emic commentator Nāgojī Bhaṭṭa.[2]

So, with all of this in mind, and in the interests of full disclosure in the context of positionality, let me categorise myself as a reader, a scholar and an interpreter of Vālmīki's grand and poetic epic treatment of the life of King Rāma of Ayodhyā. I am an American academic, and a student of Sanskrit language and literature. I grew up in New York City and completed my higher education at two of America's so-called 'Ivy League' universities, Columbia (BA) and the University of Pennsylvania (PhD). I have been researching and teaching Sanskrit and Indian literature for fifty years at the University of California at Berkeley. In the schools in which I studied before college, students—in that era—received absolutely no instruction in anything to do with Indian history, culture or civilisation, or, for that matter, those of any Asian country. It was only when, as a college sophomore chemistry student pursuing a pre-medical course, I chose to take a course on Asian civilisations that I first had an opportunity to learn about India's extraordinary history and culture. Fascinated, I began to study Sanskrit and wound up going to graduate school in the field where I began to focus my scholarly interest on the great Sanskrit epics, the *Mahābhārata* and the *Rāmāyaṇa*, and their role in both inscribing and influencing the cultures of India from antiquity to the present.

Since completing my graduate training, I have spent cumulatively some ten years in various parts of India consulting academic scholars in many fields, reading Sanskrit texts with traditionally trained paṇḍits, and teaching and lecturing in Indian colleges and universities (including Jadavpur University). As a result, I have come to have a deep understanding of both academic critical scholarship on Indian texts and traditional ways of reading and interpreting these texts; in other words, in both the etic and emic approaches. I also strive to engage my graduate students in both approaches to their subject matter by insisting that they read Sanskrit commentaries as well as academic scholarship on the texts they are researching and by consulting with both academic and traditionally trained scholars in India.

With the issues mentioned above as a preamble, let me now turn to the text itself, its nature, its form, its contents, the *work* it performs for its audiences, ancient and modern, and how one may go about reading it.

What is the *Vālmīki Rāmāyaṇa*?

Before we get into the details of the contents of poem and its meaning one might naturally want to get a clear understanding of what it is as an *object*. What I mean, simply, is that if one wishes to read the work in the original Sanskrit, what is it that one holds before his or her eyes? Well, other than live or recorded versions of the work being recited, one would generally be looking at the work in one of four forms: a manuscript, a printed edition, on a digital device or one of the minimally edited printed forms, *pothī*, that duplicate the format of manuscripts. Printed editions may be accompanied by a translation while manuscripts and some printed editions may include one or more commentaries.

Now a non-scholarly reader might naturally assume that any such textual object represents the original, unitary and authentic version of the poem. After all, the work itself makes the claim, widely accepted in traditional circles, that the entire poem was produced at one time by a single divinely inspired ṛṣi, or seer, who had been granted divine vision through which he was able to literally and directly see all of the events depicted in his creation. The seer Vālmīki then, so the text itself tells us, teaches it to two brilliant students who recite it word for word, far and wide. This telling of the tale, according to tradition, has remained unchanged down to the present day and will continue to be current among the people as long as the earth itself endures.

But nothing could be further from the truth. In fact, the very success of the poem and its unparalleled popularity, have led, over the more than two millennia since its first circulation, to a plethora of versions, sometimes called recensions, and sub-versions in every corner and every writing system of South Asia and beyond. If we take the work at its word to the effect that it was orally composed and circulated, which may or may not be literally true, then from its earliest public performance, as described in the poem's prologue, it would have begun to change in the recitations of various bards and singers of tales who would be ever more distant in time and place from the first performers. For, as we know from much more recent examples, orally composed and performed texts inevitably change to a greater or lesser extent in different performances, even by the same bard and still more so in the hands of different singers, either through failures of memory or through improvisation in response to different times, places, occasions and the reactions of particular audiences (Lord 1960).

Be this as it may, it is beyond belief that a work of this size could have been circulated orally from what is today Afghanistan to Bali without it being at some early moment in its history, committed to writing. And in fact, this was the case as countless manuscripts of the poem were widely copied and circulated throughout southern Asia, many of which, starting from around the turn of the first millennium CE, are still in circulation.

But the copying and transmission of manuscripts is also fraught with imperfection. One problem is, of course, the diligence and competence of the scribes who do the copying. Such issues are particularly weighty in the case of the scribal transmission of Sanskrit texts in India. This is because Sanskrit, although it is, for the most part, a highly conservative and grammatically regulated language, has never, unlike, say, Greek or Latin, had a single principal script in which it was universally written. Thus, as the manuscript tradition of Vālmīki's *Rāmāyaṇa* developed over time, the work came to be copied in a wide variety of regional scripts from all parts of India, from the Śāradā script of Kashmir to the Grantha and Malayalam scripts of the deep south, and many others in between. This in turn contributed to a sort of graphic game of 'telephone' in which scribes copying a manuscript from one script into another for their local readers might well make errors or changes.

As a result of this and because of the very popularity of the work itself, the poem has undergone numerous and complex textual changes which have resulted in the formation of a number of primary and secondary recensions or textual variants. Basically, there are two major versions represented, respectively, by manuscripts from northern India in northern scripts and from southern India in southern scripts including many relatively late manuscripts in the widely written and printed Devanāgarī script. The textual differences between these two large recensions are quite significant so that—in terms of a word for word, verse for verse, passage for passage comparison between the northern and southern recensions—

only about a third of the two versions are actually textually identical.

Even this north-south division does not fully reflect the textual situation of the Vālmīki *Rāmāyaṇa* as it has survived in manuscript form. For within each major recension there are further regional sub-recensions, so that there is, for example, a northwest recension, which is allied to but distinct from the so-called Bengal recension. And then, as noted already, manuscripts within the recensions and sub-recensions differ depending on the scripts in which they have been copied. So, for example, there are particularities associated with Devanāgarī manuscripts, Grantha manuscripts, Śāradā manuscripts and so on. The widely circulated, modern printed editions of the poem represent one or another of the recensions or sub-recensions. For instance, there is Gaspare Gorresio's edition of the Gauḍīya, or Bengal recension (1843–1867), Vishva Bandhu's 'Lahore' edition of the northwestern recension (1928–1947), and the numerous editions of the southern recension such as the 'Kumbakonam' edition (Krishnacharya and Vyasacharya, eds., 1911–1913) and those of the Gujarati Printing Press (Mudholkar ed., 1914–1920), the Nirnaya Sagara Press (Parab, ed., 1888), the Gita Press (1969 and 1988), and the Venkateshwara Steam Press (Śrīkṛṣṇadāsa, ed., 1935). All existing translations of the Vālmīki *Rāmāyaṇa,* with the exception of the Princeton University Press's seven-volume translation (Goldman, et al. 1984–2017) and the recent one of Bibek Debroy (2017), are of one or another of these existing published editions. These last two are English renderings of the critical edition of the poem which differs in varying degrees from its various surviving manuscripts and printed editions. Therefore, those familiar with other published editions and/or the translations based on them will note that our Princeton University Press translation departs in many places from editions and translations they may have read. For those not familiar with the critical edition or even with the concept of such an edition, I am referring here to the text-historical reconstruction of an archetype of the surviving manuscript tradition of the epic produced by the scholars of the *Rāmāyaṇa* Department of the Oriental Institute of Baroda under the direction of scholars from G.H. Bhatt to U.P. Shah between 1960 and 1975. It should be understood that the oldest surviving manuscripts of the epic are much later than the composition of the poem itself. Thus the critical edition cannot be regarded as a reconstruction of an 'original' *Rāmāyaṇa*, something that is beyond the reach of philology. Rather, the scholars compared what they considered exemplary manuscripts from the various recensions and sub-recensions and used the tools of text-historical philology to produce a text that approximates the state of the text at the time of its oldest available manuscripts.

The fact that these oldest surviving manuscripts were copied at least a millennium later than the original circulation of the poem is the consequence of the perishability of the various manuscript media used in ancient and early modern South and Southeast Asia. Sanskrit manuscripts, depending on period and region, have been written on a variety of media including prepared palm leaves, birch bark and various forms of paper. These materials have generally had relatively short life spans in the hot and moist environment of monsoon Asia. Manuscripts succumb to mould, insects, general neglect and, in some cases, even a form of pious destruction in which religious texts, like the *Rāmāyaṇa*, are sometimes consigned to bodies of water in the practice of *visarjana*, or 'release' of sacred images, icons or texts.

Thus, the plethora of textual variants and the loss of perishable manuscripts over time presents the scholar of the *Rāmāyaṇa* with a serious problem when it comes to an understanding of what the poem may have been like in its earliest stages. The core of the work appears to have been a product of the last half of the first millennium BCE, but because of the factors mentioned above, its oldest known manuscripts are dated no earlier than the twelfth or thirteenth centuries CE, leaving a period of perhaps as much as seventeen centuries from which we can recover virtually no written record of the poem.

Then too, the etic reconstruction of the *Rāmāyaṇa*'s genetic history, is naturally going to be at odds with its emic receptive history of the work. The general academic, philological and historical understanding of the poem is that it is perhaps an originally historical, orally composed, bardic poem composed by one or more bards and redactors, collectively known as Vālmīki, which first circulated in the late first millennium BCE. The work appears to be loosely based on the legend of an ancient king of the *janapada* of Kosala. Over time the poem came to be expanded by other bards and storytellers to incorporate imaginative tales of ten-headed demons, talking monkeys, flying chariots, etc., and became subject to the vagaries of oral performance and manuscript transmission from that time forward. The work's intended audience and its custodians, its commentators and the poets of later regional and sectarian versions, along with pious people who have read or hear the work recited from antiquity to modernity, however, understand the work quite differently. For them, the poem is the unitary utterance of a single, inspired seer, the ṛṣi Vālmīki, who was a contemporary of the epic's hero whose long life thus played out in the Treta Yuga, the second of the recurring four cosmic eras long before our modern age. According to this calculation then, the poem is an inerrant history of a great, ancient Indian king, an earthly incarnation of the supreme deity, who lived many hundreds of thousands of years ago and came to earth in order to destroy the forces of evil and disorder, in short, adharma, and re-establish a millennia-long kingdom of order and righteousness, or dharma. In brief, the two traditions of reading are at odds as to whether the epic is a contingent, human, poetic mixture of history and mythology, a kind of historical novel, or whether it is a chapter of divine history rendered in a new form, that of poetry. Let's explore this issue further with a discussion of ideas of genre. In brief, the question is whether the *Rāmāyaṇa* is a poetic history or a historical poem.[3]

Now, when one talks or writes about the *Rāmāyana* and its close relative the *Mahābhārata*, we tend to characterise them under the generic western term 'epic'. Indeed, the Indian critical editions of both texts describe them, almost in competition with each other, with this term. The Pune, or Bhandarkar Oriental Research Institute (BORI), critical edition of the *Mahābhārata* calls its reconstruction of that massive text 'India's Great Epic' (Sukthankar, et al. 1933–1970) while the later Baroda, or Oriental Institute of Baroda (OIB), critical edition of the *Rāmāyaṇa*, calls its text 'India's National Epic' (Bhatt and Shah, 1960–1975).[4]

In literary contexts, the term 'epic', derived from Latin and Greek terms for poetry, has long been used to describe what Dictionary.com recently defined as,

> Noting or pertaining to a long poetic composition, usually centered upon a hero, in which a series of great achievements or events is narrated in elevated style.[5]

And, when people in the west today use the term in this sense a noun, the models that come most readily to mind are works such as the ancient Greek and Latin heroic narrative poems, the *Iliad,* the *Odyssey* and the *Aeneid.*[6]

But, if we turn to Indian literary theory, it would seem that the definition of epic exemplified by the quotation above might fit a large number of works ranging from the *Mahābhārata* and the *Rāmāyaṇa*, to mahākāvyas such as the *Raghuvaṃśa* and *Śiśupālavadha.* And it is certainly the case that we speak conventionally of Vyāsa's and Vālmīki's works, which share many features in common with ancient western epic poetry, as the great epics of India. But like the west, India too has a long, rich and sophisticated history of literary classification, analysis and interpretation, including an extensive system of genre distinctions. Nevertheless, it is difficult to find a precise term in the refined and elaborate classificatory schemes of Indian literary theory, known as *sāhityaśāstra* or *alaṅkāraśāstra*, that corresponds very precisely to the western category of the epic. Thus, of the works listed above, the latter two are universally classified by Sanskrit authorities on literary criticism as belonging to the specific genre of *mahākāvya*. But, the Sanskrit lexicon of literary types, copious though it may be, does not have a single precise genre term for classifying the *Rāmāyaṇa* and the *Mahābhārata*, texts academic scholars now classify as 'epics'. Nor is it uniformly the case that these two great poems are regarded by Indian *alaṅkāraśāstrins*, or literary critics, as even belonging to the same genre.

The *Mahābhārata*, is most frequently classified as belonging to the genre of *itihāsa*, a term for a historical narrative couched mainly in poetic, or at the least, in metrical form. This is a genre that is in a number of respects hard to distinguish from the huge category of purāṇa, with many examples of which the 'epics' are highly intertextual. Thus, works in the latter genre frequently include versions of the narratives of those of the former in whole or in part while the 'epics' also include passages that replicate some of the five prescribed elements, or *pañcalakṣaṇa*, of the purāṇas. Indeed, these two genres are often clumped together in the portmanteau genre of itihāsa-purāna. The use of this composite term is further supported by the way in which a number of purāṇic texts, particularly those of a Vaiṣṇava-Bhāgavata orientation, position themselves as extensions, or *khila*s, of the *Mahābhārata*. Exemplary here is the *Harivaṃśamahāpurāṇa* which defines itself as such an appendix to the *Mahābhārata*.

But if Vyāsa's *Mahābhārata* is the prototypical work of itihāsa, Vālmīki's *Rāmāyaṇa* is cast, in its own prologue and in the general poetic tradition, as the archetypal work, indeed the very *fons et origo* of the genre of *kāvya*, poetry. One may note here a technical point that is illustrative of the traditional genre distinction between the two works. This is to be seen in the terms used in manuscripts and printed editions of the works. The individual eighteen books of the *Mahābhārata*, are called *parvan*s and their sub-chapters *adhyāya*s, terms more closely associated with purāṇas and śāstras than poems. But the seven books of the *Rāmāyaṇa* are called *kāṇḍa*s while each kāṇḍa's chapters are called *sargas*, terms generally used for the sections of long literary works. Nonetheless, these particular genre categories are not, when it comes to these works, very rigidly defined. At various points in the lengthy and complex text of the *Mahābhārata*, it defines itself as kāvya, but leaves its classification somewhat blurred, as, for example where Vyāsa, the legendary composer of the work, representing his work as inclusive of many genres, says to Lord Brahmā,

> *kṛtaṃ mayedaṃ bhagavan kāvyaṃ paramapūjitam* ||
> *brahman vedarahasyaṃ ca yac cānyat khyāpitaṃ mayā* |
> *sāṅgopaniśadānāṃ ca vedānāṃ vistarakriyā* ||
> *itihāsapurāṇānām unmeṣaṃ nirmitaṃ ca yat* |
> (*MbhC* 1.1.61cd–63ab)[7]

> I created this highly revered poem, Holy One, which expresses the secrets of the vedas, as well as other things that I have proclaimed. These are: the full explication of the vedas along with the upaniṣads and the adjunctive sciences. And I have also created here a full expansion of the itihāsas and purāṇas.

Then, too, the first literary theorists to look critically at the *Mahābhārata* and the *Rāmāyaṇa* as coherent works of poetic literature, Ānandavardhana and Abhinavagupta, the great promulgators of the *rasa–dhvani* school of alaṅkāraśāstra, are themselves ambivalent when it comes to the genre question. Although they see both texts as through-composed works of poetry unified in each case by a consistent, dominant emotive-aesthetic mood, or *rasa*, they also refer to both of them at various points as itihāsa.[8]

Before proceeding to an in-depth study of how a reader can approach the *Rāmāyaṇa*, it is important that we keep in mind a particular issue in the formulation and the reception of virtually all premodern Sanskrit texts of whatever genre.

The issue I have in mind is that of *vyutpatti*, which we might render in English as edification or cultivation.

As stated famously by Abhinavagupta, the purpose of all genres of composition is vyutpatti since all texts should contain teaching with respect to the four principal aims of human life, the so-called *caturvarga*, consisting of dharma, artha, kāma and mokṣa. But the various types or genres of text carry out their educational function in different ways. Thus, according to Abhinava, the Vedas teach those who hear or read them in the manner of a master (*prabhu*), by which he means in the fashion of a stern guru who must be revered. Itihāsa teaches in the manner of a friend (*mitra*), that is, as between equals, while kāvya teaches in the fashion of a wife (*jāyā*), which is to say, sweetly and pleasurably. In his view, then, the distinguishing feature of kāvya, or, true poetry, which sets it apart from the other genres is that it places pleasure or delight (*prīti*, *ānanda*) above its instructional and edifying function.[9]

So, if we take Abhinava's understanding of genre as our starting point and see the lover-like creation of aesthetic delight as the distinctive quality of kāvya, and the 'friendly' but comprehensive instruction in matters pertaining to the *caturvarga* as the hallmark of itihāsa,[10] then we can perhaps find in this a basis for making another kind of genre distinction between the *Rāmāyaṇa* and the *Mahābhārata*. Here we can note that the former text is rather more given to highly figured and charming descriptions of nature, flora, fauna, the seasons, etc., as well as deeply moving depictions of the sorrow experienced by its hero and heroine when separated from one another. Then, too, the two works differ sharply in their underlying emotional tone and in the ways in which they frame their narratives as mediums for vyutpatti. Vālmīki's poem is marked throughout by passages in which the emotion of grief for the loss of one's beloved is movingly displayed. Indeed, that is why the founders of the Kashmiri rasa–dhvani school of poetics argued that the principal aesthetic–emotive sentiment of the work is *karuṇa-rasa,* the sublimated emotion of *śoka*, or grief (*DhvĀlo* and *Loc* 4.5.). Indeed, for the poem's hero, the narrative ends with his suffering, yet again, the loss of his beloved Sītā as she enters the earth at the side of her mother, the Goddess Mādhavī. But his personal loss aside, the work ends on a positive note with Rāma inaugurating his legendary restoration of a millennia-long and wholly righteous reign which seems to reverse, as it were, the very degeneration of the world as it passes through the sequence of the *yugas*. For the work tells us that once Rāma finally assumed the rulership of his kingdom in the Tretā Yuga, the conditions in his realm were just like those that existed in the Kṛta Yuga (*kṛtayuge yathā VR* 1.1.73), the paradisiac era of righteousness and perfect harmony in nature as well as in society.

The *Mahābhārata*, in contrast, is a much darker text. Its central narrative is one of bitter and irremediable conflict between two factions of a royal family, leading, ultimately, to a violent civil war in which the scions of the ruling lineage slaughter one another leaving the heroes of the work bereft and despondent, their world in ruins. All of this is framed, from beginning to end, around a series of sanguinary, genocidal conflicts (Goldman 2021). So grim is the text, in fact, that the same literary śāstrins who identify *karuṇa*, the piteous emotion as the principal rasa of the *Rāmāyaṇa*, were forced to add an entirely new one, *śāntarasa*, the aestheticised emotion of revulsion for all worldly things, as a ninth to Bharatamuni's traditional list of eight in order to capture the emotional tenor of the work. Ānandavardhana thus writes of the *virasāvasāna*, 'the miserable end' of the Pāṇḍavas and their cousins the Vṛṣṇis. For, on the final journey of the Pāṇḍavas and their wife Draupadī, all of them save Yudhiṣṭhira fall dead on the path while, as for the Vṛṣṇis, Kṛṣṇa's own people, they slaughter one another in a drunken, internecine brawl (*Mbh* 16.5).

With this in mind let me turn first to the actual literary claims of the *Rāmāyaṇa*, examining them in some detail, but always keeping in mind the higher purpose, the vyutpatti, that lies imbedded in the monumental poem's poetic matrix. In this way, the *Rāmāyaṇa* becomes an exemplary tale of a noble hero who, along with his loving wife and devoted brother, come to serve as the models for at least aspirational righteousness from antiquity to the present. It serves then as both a mirror for kings and a guide to the young for how to conduct themselves in society. The *Mahābhārata*, on the other hand, is a massive cautionary tale of the moral and ethical snares that beset us in this world and a painful exhortation for us to detach ourselves from worldly things. The, at times, questionable ethics of its heroes do not make for much of a guide for conduct in general and certainly not for children in particular. At the epic's end, its author gives himself up to a kind of existential despair about the didactic effectiveness of his tragic history, its ability to serve as a primer for dharma, lamenting:

> 'I cry out with arms upraised, but no one listens to me. Righteousness is the source of both profit and pleasure. Why then is it not practiced?' (*ūrdhvabāhur viraumy eṣa na ca kaś cic chṛṇoti me | dharmād arthaś ca kāmaś ca sa kimarthaṁ na sevyate* || *Mbh* 18.5.49).

The aesthetic or literary component in the prestige and popularity of Vālmīki and the monumental epic poem ascribed to him is absolutely unique within the realm of Sanskrit poetry and poetics and, indeed, in the history of Indian literature in general. The work claims for itself the distinction of being not just a great poem but the world's very first poetic composition, which then becomes the model, source and inspiration for the entire genre of poetry (*paraṃ kavīnām ādhāraṃ VR* 1.4.20d). The long narrative poem, as it has come down to us, is provided with an extraordinary meta-poetic framing narrative that recounts how the work came to be composed and, at both the beginning and the end of the work, an account of its first performances by the bards Lava and Kuśa, who are the *protégés* and disciples of the author as well as the sons of the work's hero Rāma. The prologue, or *upodghāta*, is of particular interest as it provides an early narrative formulation of the Indian tradition's understanding of the nature of literary creation and aesthetics. That is to say that it became an element in the later, ongoing debate among the various schools of poetic theory as to what exactly constitutes the specific quality of poetry that distinguishes it from all other forms of linguistic discourse. In short, the question became that of defining what Ānandavardhana called the *kāvyasyātmā*, 'the essence or soul of poetry' (*DhvĀlo* 1.1).The episode is also the basis for the identification and celebration of Vālmīki as the Ādikavi, or First Poet, and his only known composition as the Ādikāvya, or First Poem (*VR* 1.2).

The upodghāta begins in the middle of a conversation between the forest sage Vālmīki and his guest, the celebrated heavenly seer, or *devarṣi*, Nārada. Appealing to Nārada's legendary knowledge of all things in heaven and on earth, Vālmīki asks him if there is still any truly virtuous, righteous and heroic man living in their time. In reply, the seer describes the auspicious marks and virtues of the perfect man, King Rāma of Ayodhyā. The king, a contemporary of Vālmīki, is said to be ruling a great and righteous kingdom from a capital a mere day and a half journey by horse-drawn carriage from the seer's ashram (*VR* 7.45.9–21). Rāma is also the husband of Queen Sītā, who was at that time being sheltered by Vālmīki along with her and Rāma's twin sons who are the seer's disciples. So, Vālmīki's question and his need to hear Nārada's reply seems slightly odd. Nonetheless, the divine seer then provides a very terse and dry account of Rāma's life with all of its struggles and triumphs. He concludes his account with a stereotyped recitation of the glory and perfection of Rāma's millenarian reign. Nārada's account occupies a little less than sixty Sanskrit couplets and is almost studiously devoid of literary figuration or pretension (*VR* 1.1.18–76).

Following Nārada's departure, Vālmīki, accompanied by his disciple, Bharadvāja, proceeds toward the Tamasā river for his ritual ablutions. But on the way he becomes poignantly aware of the beauties of nature that surround him and stops for a moment in rapture to watch a pair of Sarus cranes in their courting ritual. Suddenly, to his shock and horror, a tribal hunter, emerging from the forest, shoots and kills the male bird as the female cries piteously. Appalled that the hunter should have struck when the birds were distracted in the throes of passion, and filled with grief and compassion for female's suffering, the sage spontaneously curses the hunter:

> *mā niṣāda pratiṣṭhāṃ tvam agamaḥ śāśvatīḥ samāḥ* |
> *yat krauñcamithunād ekam avadhīḥ kāmamohitam* ||
>
> (*VR* 1.2.14)

Since, hunter, you killed one of this pair of cranes, distracted at the height of their passion, you shall not live very long.

Now, there is nothing especially remarkable about an angry sage cursing someone for a perceived offence in the Sanskrit literary tradition. Indeed, the curse, or *śāpa*, is an immensely common plot motif in Indian epics, plays, poems, purāṇas, etc., and the *Rāmāyaṇa* is by no means an exception to this. But this particular curse is felt to be different from all others both in its emotive content and, so the passage continues, in its form. The sage himself is puzzled by his utterance, wondering, 'Stricken with grief for this bird, what is this I have uttered?' (*śokārtenāsya śakuneḥ kim idaṃ vyāhṛtaṃ mayā. VR* 1.2.15). Then, upon reflection, he remarks upon how his words arose spontaneously from his grieving for the birds and emerged in a new and striking metrical form, suitable for musical performance. He remarks,

> *pādabaddho 'kṣarasamas tantrīlayasamanvitaḥ* |
> *śokārtasya pravṛtto me śloko bhavatu nānyathā* || (*VR* 1.2.17)
>
> Fixed in metrical quarters, each with the same number of syllables, and fit for the accompaniment of stringed and percussion instruments, this utterance that I produced in this access of *śoka*, grief, shall be called *śloka*, and nothing else.

Vālmīki's impassioned imprecation illustrates two points that are central to traditional India's conception of literary aesthetics. First, it gives voice to the idea that poetic composition is to be received and appreciated by its audience through performance, either through musical or quasi-musical recitation alone or through such recitation accompanied by fully staged visual performance. This is in keeping with the literary theorists' broad division of kāvya, literary poetry, into that which is to experienced aurally, *śravyakāvya*, or recited poetry, and that which is also to be enjoyed visually, *dṛśyakāvya*, or staged drama.

The sage's second point has proven even more critical to one of India's principal conceptions of what actually constitutes the essence or 'soul' of poetry (*kāvyasyātmā*). It is not merely a formal matter since Sanskrit composition regarded as poetic or literary may be in a variety of forms and genres and may be either *padya*, metrical, or *gadya*, prose. Rather, it is the capacity of the work to strike a particular kind of resonant chord with some profound and fundamental human emotion, in Vālmīki's case the emotion of śoka. Thus, Vālmīki's use of the common Indian cultural trope of what one might call 'the meaningful pun' links the term for grief, śoka, with the term śloka, here meaning versified poetry in general. This intimate connection between raw emotion and sublimated aesthetic response serves as a touchstone for poets and for literary theoreticians, many of whom saw the defining element of poetry to be precisely its ability to stimulate one or more of a set of particular rasas, in its intended audiences (Pollock 2016, 144–80).

After completing his ablutions, Vālmīki returns to his ashram, still pondering over the events of the morning. There he is visited by no less a personage than Lord Brahmā, the Creator, to whom he recites his newly composed śloka. The god tells him that it was through his divine inspiration that the sage produced this heartfelt and aesthetically pleasing verse. Brahmā then commissions the sage to employ his newly acquired literary powers to compose an elaborate and detailed poetic and musical account of the story of Rāma that he had earlier heard in concise, prosaic verse from Nārada. The Creator promises that, through his divine power, every event in the history of Rāma and the other figures with whom the hero has interacted and will interact in the future, will be revealed to the sage. Brahmā thus instructs Vālmīki to compose 'the holy story of Rāma fashioned into *ślokas* to delight the heart' (*kuru rāmakathāṃ puṇyāṃ ślokabaddhāṃ manoramām. VR* 1.2.34).

After composing the great poem, Vālmīki teaches it to two of his disciples, Lava and Kuśa, the abovementioned twin sons of Rāma and Sītā, who then sing the work to gatherings of sages and ultimately, before the king, their father, himself (*VR* 1.4.12–27). Noteworthy here is that the work is said to be replete with all of the classical aesthetic–emotive sentiments (*VR* 1.4.8) and, as noted above, to be the ultimate source and inspiration for all later poets.

Following the two opening sargas of the poem in which these events are described, there are two more (*VR* 1.3–4), the first of which serves as a description of how Vālmīki composed the work and a table of contents of the major episodes in the epic tale. The second of these recounts the first performances of the poem by Lava and Kuśa which delight their audience of sages. Finally, they perform the work before the king, their father who, the narrative makes clear at the very end of the long poem, has been somehow unaware until that point of their existence.

Now it appears quite obvious that in light of its content, which was clearly composed in order to provide a rationale for the poem's reputation as divinely inspired and as the origin of poetry, this upodghāta is a later addition to the fully developed work. Moreover, Vālmīki was one of the literary tradition's legendary omniscient seers whose ashram was only two days by horse carriage from the capital city of Rāma's. Thus, it stretches the limits of suspension of disbelief to think that he would have to ask Nārada as to who, in that moment of time, was a truly virtuous, righteous and powerful man, and would thus need to hear from him the tale of Rāma.

Moreover, the prologue's temporal placement in the narrative raises a number of logical and chronological difficulties. As noted above, according to the poem's *Uttarakāṇḍa*, Vālmīki knows all about Sītā's banishment by Rāma even before he takes her in to shelter her (*VR* 7.48.5–10). In addition, as we see in the *Bālakāṇḍa*, Brahmā grants the sage the ability to directly witness and retell everything that happened in Rāma's eventful life as well as in the lives of those with whom he interacts throughout the lengthy narrative (*VR* 1.2.30–34). At that very moment in which the sage is blessed by Brahmā, Vālmīki had been already fostering the banished Sītā and her twins Lava and Kuśa in his ashram for twelve years as we know from the fact that he taught it to them immediately after composing it. Then, too, the upodghāta's listing of seven of the eight classical rasas as first posited in the later *Nāṭyaśāstra*, would seem to presuppose a prior history of poetic and performative theory.[11] The section would thus appear to be later than at least the earliest iteration of Bharatamuni's great treatise.[12]

Nonetheless, leaving aside the *genetic* history of the poem—as it has come down to us in its various regional and subregional recensions—we must acknowledge that, according to the all but universal *receptive* history of the work in the Indian literary tradition, this meta-poetic legend framing the epic tale provides an authentic account of the miraculous origin of poetry of which the later poet-playwright Bhavabhūti calls 'a new incarnation of metrical composition different from the vedas' (*āmnāyād anyo nūtanaś chandasām avatāraḥ. UttRāC* following 2.5) and 'a historical work (itihāsa) that is the first transformation among men of the Absolute in the form of sound' (*prathamaṃ manuṣyeṣu śabdabrahmaṇas tādṛśaṃ vivartam itihāsam. UttRāC* following 2.5).This reinforces the tradition that no less an authority than the Creator himself, Lord Brahmā, has conferred upon Vālmīki the unique distinction of beng the First Poet.[13]

But if we leave this fascinating and important episode aside for a moment, it would be useful for us as students of comparative literature, to examine the poem itself in terms of its literary merit both within the tradition of Indian literary criticism and, on a comparative basis with other, similar works of world literature. An obvious object of comparison here would be the well-known, widely studied and frequently translated epic poems of ancient Greece, the *Iliad* and the *Odyssey*. These works, which have long been staples of the western literary canon, have in many ways established in western and international audiences a certain sense of what an epic poem is and should be. In his famous lectures on the Homeric epics delivered at Oxford in 1860 and later published as *On Translating Homer* the poet and literary critic Matthew Arnold (1896) called attention to what he saw as the Greek poet's and, perhaps by extension, all epic poetry's four principal stylistic virtues. Homer, he stated, 'is eminently rapid; that he is eminently plain and direct, both in the evolution of his thought and in the expression of it, that is, both in his syntax and in his words; that he is eminently plain and direct in the substance of his thought, that is, in his matter and ideas; and, finally that he is eminently noble.' (Arnold 1896, 10). These are qualities that western literary critics generally speaking, continue to prize.

Now although no one can really question the nobility—however one may judge that quality—of the works of Vālmīki and Vyāsa, one can hardly describe them as, rapid, or, for the most part plain or direct. To compare the Greek with the Sanskrit epics, we must first consider the relative size and scope of the texts in question.

In its standard vulgate form, the one normally read and translated today, the *Iliad* contains over fifteen thousand lines of Homeric Greek composed in dactylic hexameter. Each line thus consists of six metrical 'feet' of three syllables each for a total of eighteen syllables. The Sanskrit epics are considerably longer and more metrically diverse. The *Mahābhārata*, in its vulgate versions, runs to some two hundred thousand lines while the vulgate versions of the *Rāmāyaṇa* contain some fifty thousand lines. Both Indian poems are largely composed in the Anuṣṭubh, or śloka, meter with sixteen syllables per line, but both poems alternate this pattern with several longer meters, most commonly the Triṣṭubh meter with twenty-two syllables per line.[14] So, by this rough calculation, the *Mahābhārata* is some eight times the length of the two Homeric epics combined, while the *Rāmāyaṇa*, the shorter of the two Indian epics, is merely twice the combined length of the Greek poems. So, clearly, the qualities of rapidity and directness, in effect of brevity, that Arnold saw in Homer, would not seem to have been a concern of the Indian poets.

Then, too, we must compare the narrative breadth of the Homeric poems with that of the Indian epics. Let's take the *Iliad* again as an example. In it Homer basically restricts his narration to a period of but a few weeks toward the end of the Trojan War, although various passages in the work refer to the background and causes of the conflict and look forward to its ending and aftermath. By contrast, the Indian poets, especially Vyāsa, stretch their histories back through elaborate accounts of many generations of the ancestors of the epic characters, to the cosmic wars of the gods and the demons and ultimately back to the creation of the world itself. The central narrative events in the Indian poems are battles that last only a matter of weeks but, aside from the accounts of the long genealogical histories that precede the lives of the epic heroes and their accounts of what takes place after the central battles, they also enrich and enliven their central stories with thematically related but narratively unconnected episodes often amounting to mini-epics in themselves. The well-known *upākhyānas*, parallel histories of figures such as Śakuntalā (*Mbh* 1.62–69), Sāvitrī (*Mbh* 3.277–283), Nala (*Mbh* 3.50–77) and Rāma (*Mbh* 3.257–275) are part of the reason for the great length of the *Mahābhārata* as are numerous other shorter tales and especially the lengthy discourses on law, philosophy, kingship and many other topics in its twelfth and thirteenth books. And, although the *Rāmāyaṇa* is, of course, rather more parsimonious with its parallel tales than the longer epic, it is not completely averse to such material, as in the *Bālakāṇḍa's* elaborate accounts of the descent of the Gaṅga (*VR* 1.37–43) and the career of Viśvāmitra (*VR* 1.50–64) and the *Uttarakāṇḍa's* extensive thirty-four chapter-long narrative of the origin and genealogy of the *rākṣasas* and the career of the epic's antagonist, Rāvaṇa, a narrative that occupies a full half of the text of that book (*VR* 7.4–34) testify. This final and relatively brief kāṇḍa also contains a number of cautionary tales of earlier kings and their tragic fates.

As to the quality of 'directness' that Arnold ascribes to Homer, there are again some noteworthy differences. As the great literary critic Erich Auerbach notes, Homer's narrative is characterised by his 'need for an externalization of phenomena in terms perceptible to the senses' (Auerbach 2003, 6). In practice we see that the Greek poet's descriptions are very detailed and graphic in ways that we, as an audience, can easily understand in terms of our innate feeling for the ordinary human sensorium. Vālmīki, on the other hand, is often intent on describing his characters and events in grandly hyperbolic terms, far beyond our day-to-day experience, in order to create in his audience a sense of awe at the grandeur of his characters that is almost beyond imagination. Let me illustrate this with two examples, one from the *Iliad* and one from the *Rāmāyaṇa*, of two passages describing single combat, or what the Sanskrit poets call *dvandvayuddha*.

The first, drawn from the fifth book of the *Iliad*, in Fitzgerald's translation, describes the end of the duel between the Greek warrior Diomedes and the Trojan prince Pandaros. Diomedes, wounded by Pandaros's arrow, parries a spear throw and then hurls his own spear in return.

> At this he made his cast,
> his weapon being guided by Athena
> to cleave Pandaros' nose beside the eye
> and shatter his white teeth: his tongue
> the brazen spearhead severed, tip from root,
> then plowing on came out beneath his chin.
> He toppled from the car, and all his armour
> clanged on him, shimmering. The horses
> quivered and shied away; but life and spirit
> ebbed from the broken man, he lay still. (Fitzgerald 1974, 118–119)[15]

Aside from the reference to the goddess Athena guiding Pandaros's arrow, the description is perfectly naturalistic, even graphically so, as we visualise, almost feel, the agonising and anatomically precise passage of the bronze spearhead through Pandaros's flesh and bone. There is no hyperbole and very little figuration. The poet achieves his very powerful effect with the use of only two simple, descriptive adjectives, 'brazen' and 'white'.

Compare this passage with Vālmīki's description of the conclusion of the duel between Rāma and the gargantuan rākṣasa prince Kumbhakarṇa in our translation from the sixth book of the *Rāmāyaṇa*.

> Then Rāma took up the arrow of Indra, sharp, beautifully fletched and perfect. It shone like the rays of the sun. It had the speed of Māruta, the wind god and it resembled the staff of Brahmā or Kāla, the ender of all things. Its fletching was gorgeous with diamonds and *jāmbūnada* gold, and it shone like the blazing sun or fire. It had the striking power of great Indra's *vajra* or a thunderbolt; and Rāma loosed it at the night-roaming *rākṣasa*. Set in motion by Rāghava's arm, the arrow sped on its way, lighting up the ten directions with its inherent splendor. Its appearance was as brilliant as that of Agni Vaiśvānara, undimmed by smoke, and its power was equal to that of mighty Śakra's thunderbolt. With it, Rāma severed the *rākṣasa* lord's head—huge as a mountain peak, its fangs bared, its gorgeous earrings swinging wildly—just as, long ago, Indra, smasher of citadels, severed the head of Vṛtra. Struck off by Rāma's arrow, the *rākṣasa's* head, which resembled a mountain, fell. It smashed the gates of the buildings on the main thoroughfares and knocked down the lofty rampart. Finally, the enormous *rākṣasa*, who looked like Himālaya, fell into the sea, the abode of waters. There it crushed crocodiles, shoals of huge fish, and serpents before it entered the earth. (Goldman, Sutherland Goldman, van Nooten 2009, 298–99)[16]

The two passages describe similar events. But, where Homer is spare and direct, Vālmīki shrouds the simple action he is describing in a dense cloud of adjectives and similes, concluding the episode with grand hyperbole as the giant demon's severed head and body, in falling, cause massive destruction to the city of Laṅkā and even among denizens of the deep. He makes no effort to describe the injury to the rākṣasa's body, but deploys his descriptive powers to grandly render a portrait of the arrow and its power and the immensity of Kumbhakarṅa's body.

Even when Homer wishes to use our kinaesthetic sense to emphasise the might of the warriors of the heroic age of the Trojan war, he does so with considerable restraint so that, as in the following passage, our awe is tempered by the modesty of his exaggeration. So, for example, when he says,

> Tydides raised a stone—a mighty weight,
> Such as no two men living now could lift;
> But he, alone, could swing it round with ease. (Bryant 1871, 148)[17]

we can easily imagine the weight of such a stone and the strength that would be required to lift it. We understand that the poet is telling us that his characters belonged to a vanished heroic age in which men were at least twice as powerful as the men of the poet's own time, but not so mighty as to be beyond the reach of our sensory imagination as when we might ask a friend to help lift an object too heavy for us to lift alone.

But in Vālmīki's poem, warriors routinely uproot huge trees and tear off entire mountaintops to use as weapons and, when it comes to describing the weight of Lord Śiva's mighty bow, which Rāma easily lifts and breaks, he tells us that five thousand tall and muscular men were barely able to drag it into the arena in an eight-wheeled casket (*VR* 1.66.4). We cannot, from our own sense experience, really comprehend the weight of such a thing; nor are we intended to. Rather, we are meant to marvel at the literally unimaginable power of the poet's divine hero.

Then, too, we might find instructive the types of description that the two poets employ. Homer presents a very extensive, detailed and much-discussed description of the shield that the Greek blacksmith-divinity Hephaestus crafts for Achilles at the urging of the hero's mother, the goddess Thetis. It is an example of what the Greek writers on poetics call *ekphrasis*, or dense visual description, something like what Indian alaṅkāraśāstrins call *svabhāvokti* or *jāti*, and it is, one might say, rather painterly, if not to say almost cinematic, in its effect.

Here is only a relatively brief portion of the long description of the shield from Butler's translation of the eighteenth book of the *Iliad*:

> He wrought also a fair fallow field, large and thrice ploughed already. Many men were working at the plough within it, turning their oxen to and fro, furrow after furrow. Each time that they turned on reaching the headland a man would come up to them and give them a cup of wine, and they would go back to their furrows looking forward to the time when they should again reach the headland. The part that they had ploughed was dark behind them, so that the field, though it was of gold, still looked as if it were being ploughed–very curious to behold. He wrought also a field of harvest corn, and the reapers were reaping with sharp sickles in their hands. Swathe after swathe fell to the ground in a straight line behind them, and the binders bound them in bands of twisted straw. There were three binders, and behind them there were boys who gathered the cut corn in armfuls and kept on bringing them to be bound: among them all the owner of the land stood by in silence and was glad. The servants were getting a meal ready under an oak, for they had

> sacrificed a great ox, and were busy cutting him up, while the women were making a porridge of much white barley for the labourers' dinner. He wrought also a vineyard, golden and fair to see, and the vines were loaded with grapes. The bunches overhead were black, but the vines were trained on poles of silver. He ran a ditch of dark metal all round it, and fenced it with a fence of tin; there was only one path to it, and by this the vintagers went when they would gather the vintage. Youths and maidens all blithe and full of glee, carried the luscious fruit in plaited baskets; and with them there went a boy who made sweet music with his lyre, and sang the Linus-song with his clear boyish voice. He wrought also a herd of horned cattle. He made the cows of gold and tin, and they lowed as they came full speed out of the yards to go and feed among the waving reeds that grow by the banks of the river. Along with the cattle there went four shepherds, all of them in gold, and their nine fleet dogs went with them. Two terrible lions had fastened on a bellowing bull that was with the foremost cows, and bellow as he might they haled him, while the dogs and men gave chase: the lions tore through the bull's thick hide and were gorging on his blood and bowels, but the herdsmen were afraid to do anything, and only hounded on their dogs; the dogs dared not fasten on the lions but stood by barking and keeping out of harm's way. (Butler 1952)[18]

What a marvellously detailed and visual description of the artisan's work this is. Let us compare it with Vālmīki's description of the terrifying arrow of Lord Brahmā that Rāma employs in order to finally kill the powerful rākṣasa lord Rāvaṇa.

> Reminded by Mātali's words, Rāma took up a blazing arrow that, as he did so, made a hissing sound like that of a snake. Presented to him earlier by the powerful and blessed seer Agastya,

> it was a gift of Brahmā. It was a mighty arrow, unfailing in battle. Brahmā, whose power is immeasurable, had fashioned it long ago for the sake of Indra and had presented it to that lord of the gods, who was eager to conquer the three worlds. Pavana, the wind god, resided in its feathers. Agni, the purifier, and Sūrya, bringer of light, were in its arrowhead. Its shaft was made of all of space, and the mountains Meru and Mandara lent it their weight. Radiant with its splendour, beautifully fletched, and adorned with gold, it was fashioned with the blazing energy of all the elements, and it was as brilliant as Sūrya, bringer of light. It looked like the smoking fire at the end of a cosmic age and glistened like a venomous snake. It could instantaneously shatter hosts of chariots, elephants, and horses. It could smash gateways, together with their iron beams, and even mountains. Its shaft drenched with the blood of many different creatures and smeared with their marrow, was truly frightful. Hard as adamant and roaring deafeningly, it was terrifying in every sort of battle. Dreadful, hissing like a serpent, it inspired terror in all beings. It was fearsome and looked like Yama. In battle, it provided a never-ending supply of food to flocks of vultures and adjutant storks as well as *rākṣasas* and packs of jackals. Fletched with the various feathers of Garuḍa—beautiful and variegated—it brought joy to the monkey chiefs and despair to the *raksasas*. That ultimate arrow, which robbed one's enemies of their glory but brought joy to oneself, was to encompass the destruction of that menace to the Ikṣvākus and indeed to all the worlds. (Goldman, Sutherland Goldman, and van Nooten 2009, 437; (*VR* 6.97.3–13))

Note that Homer takes us away from the shield *per se* as an object, an article of military equipment, with his dense descriptions of pastoral scenes almost as if he were an art historian writing an appreciation of Hephaestus's craftmanship. In his thick description of the various scenes emblazoned on the shield he does not use a single simile or any other specific rhetorical figure. Vālmīki, in contrast, focuses hyperbolically on a description of Rāma's arrow as a destructive weapon, highlighting its immense, supernatural and terrifying innate power by characteristically intensifying his effect with numerous similes.

Passages such as these illustrate an extremely salient characteristic of the *Rāmāyaṇa* and one which becomes very common in many genres of Indian literature. This is the poet's extraordinary penchant for rhetorical figuration which is manifest in his work's virtually innumerable examples of simile (*upamā*) and metaphor (*rūpaka*), figures which depend on comparison. Although the work is rather parsimonious in its use of some of the more elaborate figures of sound (*śabdālaṅkāra*) and sense (*arthālaṅkāra*) such as are found in later, more ornate poetry its author or authors seem all but unable to describe any object of sight, sound or touch, whether it is a person, a place, an animal, a feature of the landscape or anything else without making it also the object of one or more comparisons. Similes are generally of two types, sensory or mythological. In the former, an object of sight or sound is compared to some other sight or sound usually on a grandly exaggerated level while the *upamāna* or object of comparison, many of which are stereotyped, is something conventionally beautiful or terrifying, etc. Thus, a person's face will be compared to the moon or, if the person is suffering or unhappy, to the moon occluded by clouds or an eclipse. A wounded warrior will often be compared to either a *kiṃśuka* or *śiṃśapa* tree with their red blossoms or perhaps to a mountain coloured with its red minerals. In many cases the poet resorts to the technique of *mālopamā*, 'garland simile' in which a person or object is compared to many *upamānas*.

Mythical similes too are very plentiful as in examples where a warrior's striking down his foe is likened to Indra striking down the *asura* Vṛtra or a king surrounded by his ministers is compared to Brahmā surrounded by the *devas*, etc. In order to fully appreciate such figures, the reader or listener must be broadly familiar with Indian mythology, religion and even philosophy.

Metaphor too is woven densely across the fabric of the poem. On the simplest level, this figure is found everywhere in the epithets constantly applied to the story's large cast of characters. This is widely seen in the ubiquitous practice of using animals associated with strength, virility and courage as metaphors for heroes. These include bulls, lions, tigers, elephants and so on. In this way the poet can fill his verses with such constructions as *puruṣarṣabha*, 'bull among men', and even such striking compounds as *kapikuñjara*, 'elephant among monkeys'. Then too he is adept in the construction of elaborate and thoroughgoing metaphors (*samastavasturūpaka*), in which a complex object such as a battlefield or a river can be compared, feature by feature, with some other such feature such as a river of a woman. Examples of these various rhetorical tours de force, are given below. The point is that what with its repeated passages of elaborate description of landscapes, cityscapes, forests, oceans, rivers and its major characters, the poem creates a richly textured and imagined world of its own into which its intended audience is drawn.

But, again, while audiences brought up on and accustomed to the aesthetics of the western epics such as the *Iliad* with its rapid pace and its other qualities catalogued by Arnold may find unabridged translations of Vālmīki slow and difficult going, this is not to be held up (as some have done) as a criticism of his poem. Rather, it is a symptom of a certain kind of narrow-mindedness that may restrict one's appreciation of extraordinary works of art produced in cultures other than that with one is familiar. The critic of the masterworks of world literature should not be a *kūpamaṇḍūka*, 'a frog in a well'.

That said, there are a number of other important issues for us as students of comparative literature to consider when trying to understand how Vālmīki's monumental work functions as literature. But aside from comparison with other works, Indian and western, we must of course evaluate the quality of any literary production in the context of the aesthetic canons of the culture in which and for which it is created. So, let me turn now to a consideration of the actual aesthetics of the *Rāmāyaṇa* in light of what come to be established as the norms of *sāhityaśāstra,* the Indian science of literary criticism.

What then, finally, is the actual literary quality of the *Rāmāyaṇa*? That judgment, leaving aside the two extremes of, on the one hand, the extravagant and uncritical praise often heaped upon the work because of its legendary prestige as the First Poem and its religious significance and, on the other hand, negative critiques based on western literary prejudices, is perforce somewhat mixed. For, although the epic is regarded as the source and inspiration for the two most prestigious genres of Sanskrit poetry, the mahākāvya and *nāṭaka*, it differs from them in a number of important respects. And here, we must revert for a bit to the earlier discussion of genre. The long narrative poems, plays and other celebrated genres of classical Sanskrit poetry are for the most part wholly aesthetically oriented pieces composed by a single, historical poet normally on a relatively narrow theme and in which great effort is put into elaborate poetic figures of sound and sense (śabdālaṅkāra and arthālaṅkāra).

The *Rāmāyaṇa*, as I mentioned earlier, is not simply a kāvya, a piece whose goal is to delight the aesthetic sense of the educated connoisseur of fine poetry[19] (*sahṛdayahṛdayāhlādakārin*). The work is also an itihāsa, or history, and this fact places certain constraints upon its author that need not apply to the composer of what one might call 'pure kāvya'. For example, one of the obligations of a historian or chronicler in the Indian tradition is to provide for his or her intended audience a sort of encyclopaedic account of situations and events. In order to discharge this obligation, the poet, for the sake of verisimilitude and to create rich sense of place, etc., frequently resorts to the creation of detailed lists and catalogues of characters, genealogies, weapons, flora and fauna, etc. Vālmīki is particularly fond of such elements. Some examples are the listing of the principal monkey leaders arrayed before Laṅkā, which occupies three sargas comprising one hundred and eleven verses in the *Yuddhakāṇḍa* (*VR* 6.17–19), the list of the names of the brahmans who come to felicitate Rāma on his consecration (*VR* 7.1.2–5), lists of plants and animals,[20] and lists of the weapons used by the *rākṣasas*.[21] Although such catalogues are seen as part of the chronicler's task and can lend a kind of dense descriptive richness to some passages, it is rather difficult to appreciate or to render them in poetic form so that they might appeal to a more modern literary sensibility. By the same token, many of the descriptions of individual duels in the *Yuddhakāṇḍa* are often extremely formulaic and repetitive, which also violates one of the general prohibitions against repetitiveness or redundancy, *paunaruktyam*, which is classified as a *kāvyadośa* or poetic flaw in the treatises on poetics.[22]

One must also understand that the poetic narrative of the career of Rāma, shaped and honed by the Ādikavi, has its origins in the tradition of bardic tales, which are largely oral-formulaic in style (Lord 1960). Thus, we see that a considerable portion of the text consists of repeated formulae. This often takes the form of stock epithets for various characters, some of which, such as *kausalyānandavardhanaḥ*, 'increaser of the joy of Kausalyā', may occupy an entire quarter of a verse, while others betray the poet's fondness for echoing, etymological play as in phrases such as *lakṣmaṇo lakṣmisaṃpannaḥ*, 'Lakṣmaṇa, endowed with auspicious marks', *rāmo ramayatāṃ varaḥ*, 'Rāma, foremost of those who cause delight' and *rāvano lokarāvaṇaḥ*, 'Rāvaṇa who makes the world cry out'.

One particular formulaic feature of the *Rāmāyaṇa* involves the way in which the poet marks the change of speakers in the narrative. As is well known, the Sanskrit epics and purāṇas are structured as series of complex, emboxed dialogues in which most if not all of the text is represented as direct address on the part of its characters. Many of these texts, such as the *Mahābhārata* and the purāṇas, mark the change from the words of one speaker to those of the next by interpolating little cues outside the metrical fabric of the narrative, something like one would see in the script of a play. In these texts then, in transitions from one speaker to another, we see such phrases such as *arjuna uvāca*, 'Arjuna said', or *ṛṣaya ūcuḥ*, 'the seers said', before the speeches of the texts' respective characters. Vālmīki, however, incorporates these markers of the change of speaker into the poetic text itself, which fills the work with numerous, formulaic lines of the type *tasya tad vacanaṃ śrutvā idam vacanam abravīt*, 'Having heard that speech of his, he spoke this speech'. Such dull, repetitive sequences as this certainly diminish the poetic effect of many passages. Then, too, because of its formulaic origins and because its actual language, sometimes referred to as *ārṣa* (vedic or epic Sanskrit), does not correspond precisely to the grammatical rules set down by Pāṇini, the poem, in its various recensions, has a considerable number of grammatical forms that would be regarded as solecisms by *vaiyākaraṇas*, or traditional grammarians, as well as rhetorical deficiencies that would be seen as poetic *doṣas*, or flaws, by the alaṃkāraśāstrins. Finally, as the monumental poem seems to have grown over time, it is generally recognised that much of its first and seventh books appear to be of a later date than the five central kāṇḍas and their poetical language is often marked by less refinement than that encountered in books two through six.[23]

As noted above, one should also take seriously and keep in mind the *Rāmāyaṇa*'s description of itself as a work designed and suitable for musical performance. Traditionally, its audiences experienced the work not visually, from a printed page but rather aurally in either a genuinely musical or, more commonly, through one of the common *gānarīti*-s or modes of chanting, which vary from region to region. Consumption of the work in this form—whether as part of a short recitation of a formal *pārāyaṇa*,[24] a ritualised recitation of the whole poem—enables the audience to enjoy and participate in the experience on both an aesthetic and spiritual level. In this way the auditory experience may minimise or eliminate difference in the reception of the poem's various sections, whether they consist of highly figured description, simple narrative or dry catalogues of characters or realia.

That said, however, much of the text is quite densely and beautifully figured, especially where Vālmīki shows his remarkable talent for providing fine, haunting or even ghastly passages filled with striking similes and metaphors. Examples of this abound throughout the poem, including in its first and last books. One of the more striking ones is the richly figured and pathetic description of the heroine Sitā in her miserable and seemingly hopeless state as a captive of the brutal Rāvaṇa as she is first spied by Hanumān:

> Then he[Hanumān] saw a woman clad in a soiled garment and surrounded by *rākṣasa* women. She was gaunt with fasting. She was dejected and she sighed repeatedly. She looked like the shining sliver of the waxing moon. Her radiance was lovely; but with her beauty now only faintly discernible, she resembled a flame of fire occluded by thick smoke. She was clad in a single, fine, yellow garment, now much worn. Covered with dirt and lacking ornaments, she resembled a pond without lotuses. Ashamed, tormented by grief, disconsolate, and suffering, she looked like the constellation Rohiṇī occluded by the planet Mars. She was dejected, her face covered with tears. She was emaciated through fasting. She was depressed and given over to sorrow. Brooding constantly, she was obsessed with her grief. No longer seeing the people dear to her but only the hosts of *rākṣasa* women, she was like a doe cut off from her herd and surrounded by a pack of hounds. She had a single braid—like a black serpent—falling down her back. Deserving only happiness and unaccustomed to calamity, she was consumed with sorrow ... Sītā's face was like the full moon; her eyebrows were beautiful; her breasts were lovely and full. With her radiance that lady banished the darkness from all directions. Her hair was jet black; her lips like *bimba* fruit. Her waist was lovely, and her posture was perfect. Her eyes were like lotus petals, and she looked like Rati, wife of Manmatha, god of love. That lovely woman—as cherished by all

> living things as is the radiance of the full moon—was seated on the ground like an ascetic woman practicing austerities. Sighing constantly, that timorous woman resembled the daughter-in-law of a serpent lord. By virtue of the vast net of sorrow spread over her, her radiance was dimmed like that of a flame of fire obscured by a shroud of smoke. She was like a blurred memory or a fortune lost. She was like faith lost or hope dashed, like success undermined by catastrophe or intellect dulled. She was like a reputation lost through false rumors. She was distraught at being prevented from rejoining Rāma and anguished by her abduction by the *rākṣasa*. That delicate, fawn-eyed woman was looking about here and there. Her sorrowful face with its black-tipped eyelashes was covered with a flood of tears. She sighed again and again. Dejected, covered with dirt and grime, and devoid of ornaments—though she was worthy of them—she resembled the light of the moon, the king of stars, obscured by a black storm cloud. As he examined Sītā closely, Hanumān's mind was once more afflicted with uncertainty; for she seemed barely discernible, like some vedic text once learned by heart but now nearly lost through lack of recitation. It was only with great difficulty that Hanumān was able to recognise Sītā without her ornaments, just as one might make out the sense of a word whose meaning had been changed through want of proper usage. (Goldman and Sutherland Goldman 1996, 154–55)[25]

In this brief but moving passage the poet creates a dark mood of grief supported by some twenty-two striking similes that paint a compelling portrait of a noble and beautiful woman under a shroud of desolation and sorrow. And here is the poet's bravura description of moonrise over the splendid city of Laṅkā:

> Then the wise monkey saw the brilliant, many-rayed moon in the middle of the sky, spreading around it a great canopy of

> brilliance. It resembled a lusty bull roaming his pen. And he watched the cool-rayed moon as it rose, ending the sorrows of all the world, causing the sea to rise, and illuminating all beings. The splendor that on earth is reflected in Mount Mandara and at evening is reflected upon the sea, the splendor that in the waters is reflected in the lotus now shone forth reflected in the beautiful moon, bringer of night. Like a *haṃsa* in a silver cage or a lion in a cave on Mount Mandara, like a hero mounted on a haughty elephant, so did the moon shine forth in the sky. Rising like a sharp-horned bull, like a great white mountain with its lofty peak, like an elephant whose tusks are bound with gold, the moon shone forth, its form fully revealed. The blessed, heavenly evening was luminous, its darkness banished by the rising of the brilliant moon; its danger—the flesh-eating of the *rākṣasas*—increased; its troubles—lovers' quarrels—now banished. (Goldman and Sutherland Goldman 1996, 122)[26]

But Vālmīki is not only adept at representing beauty whether in a person or the environment. He can also turn his flair for simile and metaphor to more disturbing matters. Here is the work's extended and ghastly metaphor of the gory battlefield before the walls of Laṅkā, in which he plays on the familiar trope of the thick description of a lovely pool or river to shock our sensibilities with a vision of the horrors of war:

> Indeed, the battleground resembled a river. Masses of slain heroes formed its banks, and shattered weapons, its great trees. Torrents of blood made up its broad waters, and the ocean to which it flowed was Yama, the god of death. Livers and spleens made up its deep mud, scattered entrails its waterweeds. Severed heads and trunks made up its fish, pieces of limbs, its grass. It was crowded with vultures in place of flocks of *haṃsas*, and it was swarming with adjutant storks instead of *sārasa* cranes. It was covered with fat in place of foam, and the cries of the

> wounded took the place of its gurgling. It was not to be forded by the faint of heart. Truly, it resembled a river at the end of the rains, swarming with *haṃsas* and *sārasa* cranes. (Goldman, Sutherland Goldman, and van Nooten 2009, 247)[27]

And here is the strangely erotic metaphor of the Narmadā river as an amorous woman:

> The ten-faced bull among *rākṣasas* descended quickly from the Puṣpaka [flying palace]. Then, just as one might enter the embrace of a lovely and beloved woman, he immersed himself in the Narmadā, the foremost of rivers, which had blossoming trees for a chaplet, a pair of *cakravākas* for breasts, broad banks for hips, a line of *haṃsas* for a lovely girdle, a body smeared with pollen, the foam of the water for a white mantle, a plunge into its waters for an embrace, and blooming lotuses for lovely eyes. Afterwards, seated on its charming bank, which was adorned with all kinds of flowers, the lord of the *rākṣasas*, together with his ministers, took pleasure in the sight of the Narmadā. (Goldman and Sutherland Goldman 2017, 306–307)[28]

But apart from and beyond Vālmīki's extraordinary facility with poetic figures, especially his brilliant use of *upamā*, simile, and *rūpaka*, metaphor, there is his ability to suffuse his poem with and to instil in the hearts of his audiences the profound emotions of grief, separation and loss. Consider the following brief monologue in which Rāma gives voice to his sorrow and longing in his separation from his beloved Sītā:

> They say that grief diminishes with the passage of time. But bereft as I am of the sight of my beloved, mine only increases day by day. I do not suffer because my beloved is so far away, nor even because she has been abducted. This alone is the source of all my grief: her youth is slipping away. Blow, breeze, where my beloved stays. Touch her and then touch me. For the

> touching of our limbs now depends on you, as on the moon depends the meeting of our glances. And this, too, like poison once swallowed, and lodged in my heart, brings torment to my every limb, that, as my darling was being carried off, she must have cried out to me, 'Alas! My protector!' Night and day my body is consumed by the fire of love, whose fuel is my separation from her and whose towering flames are my constant brooding on her. (Goldman, Sutherland Goldman, and van Nooten 2009, 133–34)[29]

We must recall that, in the meta-poetic framing narrative of the *Rāmāyaṇa* the impetus to create poetry derives ultimately from emotion, the transformation of śoka into śloka. According to the theory of rasa as expounded by Bharatamuni and transformed by later authors, all of us are born with a fixed set of fundamental emotions, the so-called *sthayībhāvas* such as love, sorrow, fear, disgust, etc., which carry over in our psychological makeup from our experiences in innumerable prior births. Each of these emotions is related to, but different from, a corresponding rasa, a blissful aesthetic sublimation of that *bhāva*, or emotion. What is particularly striking here is that, for Vālmīki, or at any rate the author of the upodghāta, the emotion to first inspire the creative process from bhāva to rasa, is that of śoka, grief. So as the great theorist of rasa-dhvani, Abhinavagupta understands it, the Ādikavi did not himself experience grief *per se*. That raw emotion belonged to the surviving female krauñca bird alone. What Vālmīki experienced was the aesthetic distillate of that grief, which is the karuṇarasa, and it is this that the poet makes the principal emotive–aesthetic experience, the *pradhānarasa*, of his work.[30] This is established and continually refreshed by the poem's recurrent passages in which characters, human, simian and even demonic, bitterly lament the separation and loss of their beloved mates. Moving examples of this can be found in many fine passages such as Tārā's lament for her slain husband, the monkey lord Vālin (*VR* 4.23.1–16), Rāma's heartfelt grieving at Lake Pampā (*VR* 4.1.1–46), and on the seashore for his lost love (*VR* 6.5.4–20), and the heart-rending lamentations of Rāvaṇa's wives and his chief Queen Mandodarī's for their slain lord (*VR* 6.98.1–2 and 6.99.1–29).

All of this works powerfully together toward the shocking but aesthetically syntonic emotional ending of the work. For at the ends of the epic's two final kāṇḍas, Sītā, having survived her abduction and imprisonment at the hands of Rāvaṇa and her ordeal by fire, is reunited with Rāma yet a second time after her twelve-year period of banishment. The queen—even as she takes an oath of fidelity to her husband—chooses to enter the earth by the side of her mother, the earth goddess Mādhavī, leaving Rāma desolate and raging at their final parting in this world (*VR* 7, Appendix I, No. 13, lines 1–11).

The pre-eminence of the emotion of grief and the aesthetic experience of karuṇa, compassion, in the scholarly understanding of the nature of great poetry established in the *Rāmāyaṇa* came to be so pervasive that, centuries after the composition of the *Rāmāyaṇa*, the poet-playwright Bhavabhūti, in his drama the *Uttararāmacarita*, which is based on the episode of the banishment of Sītā, has one of his characters exclaim,

eko rasaḥ karuṇa eva nimittabhedād
bhinnaḥ pṛthakpṛthag ivāśrayate vivartān |
āvartabudbudataraṅgamayān vikārān
ambho yathā salilam eva hi tat samastam || *UttRāC* 3.47

There is only one rasa and that is karuṇa, which, because of transient modifications, appears to be divided into various kinds just as water which, although it may take the forms of whirlpools, bubbles and waves, is still, really all just water.

So, we see that Vālmīki's immortal poem, in its various recensions, even if not poetic in its every verse, has in many ways fully lived up to the upodghāta's boast that it would be both and source and inspiration, both formally and thematically, for major genres of Indian poetry, whether in Sanskrit, Prakrit or regional languages. And it has given rise to poems, plays, puppet theatre, folk plays, dance forms, cinema and television series in every language and artistic medium of southern Asia extending far beyond India into the literary and performative cultures of mainland and insular Southeast Asia and even into Central and East Asia. And, thus, two striking predictions made in the poem's prologue have proven to come true.

The first is Lord Brahmā's vow:

yāvat sthāsyanti girayaḥ saritaś ca mahītale |
tāvad rāmāyaṇakathā lokeṣu pracariṣyati || *VR* 1.2.35

As long as the mountains and rivers shall endure upon the earth, so long will the tale of the *Rāmāyaṇa* remain current among the people.

The second is that of the sages who formed the poem's first audience:

āścaryam idam ākhyānaṃ muninā saṃprakīrtitam |
paraṃ kavīnām ādhāraṃ samāptaṃ ca yathākramam ||
VR 1.4.20

This wondrous tale the sage sang forth and completed in perfect sequence shall henceforth be the fundamental source for all poets.

Notes

1. Barthes, 1968, 67.
2. As an example of how the aesthetic acculturation and literary expectations of an emic and an etic can condition their judgement of a work, consider the critical appraisal of two translators of the Rāmāyaṇa to the poem's Sundarakāṇḍa. K.R. Srinavasa Iyengar in his 1982 translation of that book, which he entitled *The Epic Beautiful*, argued that the book was the very essence of literary beauty. Contrast this with the British translator Ralph Griffith who noted in his 1873 translation of the epic of the book that, 'To a European taste it (the Sundarakāṇḍa) is the most intolerably tedious of the whole poem, abounding in repetition, overloaded description and long and useless speeches which impede the action of the poem. On this see Goldman, R. and Sutherland Goldman, S. 1996, 21.
3. For a more elaborate discussion of this issue in regard to both Sanskrit epics, see Goldman 2018.
4. The BORI critical edition of the *Mahābhārata* is hereafter referred to as MBh and that of the OIB edition of the *Rāmāyaṇa* as VR.
5. Dictionary.com Unabridged, s.v. 'epic', 2021, https://www.dictionary.com/browse/epic.
6. Of course, outside literary discourse the term has come to be popularly used as an adjective to indicate anything that the user regards as outstanding or remarkable. An example might be, 'an epic cricket test', and so on.
7. *MbhC=Mahābhārata* (Chitrashala Press 1929). *Mbh*1, App. 1.1, lines 13–16, v.l. *nimiṣam*, 'contraction,' for *nirmitam*.
8. See *Dhyanyālokalocana* on *Dhyanyāloka* 1.5 (Tripathi 1963)—hereafter referred to as *Loc* and *DhvĀlo* respectively. Ānandavardhana also refers to the *Mahābhārata* here as 'a śāstra connected with the grace of beauty (*chāyā*) of poetry' (*śāstrarūpe kāvyacchāyānvayinī*). The great playwright Bhavabhūti, too, in his *Uttararāmacarita*, refers to the *Rāmāyana* as an itihāsa:

   atha bhagavān prācetasaḥ prathamaṃ manuṣyeṣu śabdabrahmaṇas tādṛśaṃ vivartam itihāsaṃ rāmāyaṇaṃ praṇināya |

   (*UttaRāC* after 2.5)

Then, the blessed son of Pracetas (Vālmīki), for the first time among men, composed such a history, the *Rāmāyaṇa* which is really but a modified form of the Supreme Spirit as Speech.

9. *Loc* on *DhvĀlo* 1.1 (Tripathi 1963, 66):

   śrotṛṇāṃ ca vyutpattiprītī yady api staḥ ... tathāpi tatra prītir eva pradhānam. anyathā prabhusammitebhyo vedādibhyo mitrasammitebhyaś cetihāsādibhyo vyutpattihetubhyaḥ ko 'sya kāvyarūpasya vyutpattihetor jāyāsammitatvalakṣaṇo viśeṣa iti pradhānyenānanda evoktaḥ. caturvargavyutpatter api cānanda eva pāryantikaṃ mukhyaṃ phalam.

10. This is also in keeping with the Mbh's boast that it contains everything there is to be known about the caturvarga. Cf. *Mbh* 1.56.33.

    dharme cārthe ca kāme ca mokṣe ca bharatarṣabha |
    yad ihāsti tad anyatra yan nehāsti na tat kvacit ||

11. *VR* 1.4.8:

    hāsyaśṛṅgārakāruṇyaraudravīrabhayānakaiḥ |
    bībhatsādirasair yuktaṃ kāvyam etad agāyatām ||

    Note that, although the text omits *adbhutarasa*, the sentiment of wonder, from the classical list, it does, however place the term *ādi*, 'etc.', at the end of the list, suggesting that the author was aware of that eighth *rasa* but omitted its mention *metri causa*.

12. Pollock 2016.
13. *ādyaḥ kavir asi* (*UttRāC* following 2.5).
14. The *Mahābhārata* also contains a few prose passages in *adhyāyas* 3 and 4 of its *Ādiparvan*.
15. *Iliad* 5.359–268.
16. *VR* 6.55.120—125.
17. *Iliad* 5.302–304.
18. *Iliad* 18.https://www.gutenberg.org/files/2199/2199-h/2199-h.htm#chap18
19. Such a refined critic or connoisseur is called a *sahṛdaya*, literally, 'a person with a heart' in the *DhvĀlo*.
20. As for example at *VR* 6.30.3–5.
21. As for example at *VR* 6.64.3–4.
22. It is interesting to note that on the numerous occasions where the poet uses two or more seemingly synonymous terms, names or epithets in

a verse or a passage the commentators on the epic will often argue for small differences in meaning among the terms in an effort to absolve Vālmīki of this charge of paunaruktyam. A simple example of this common phenomenon can be seen at *VR* 7.7.17–18 where the poet uses two synonymous terms for 'arrow', *bāna* and *iśu*, in the passage describing a battle. The commentator Varadarāja finds this disturbing and cites the Vaijayantī lexicon, which says that one meaning of the former term refers to a specific type of arrow that lacks fletching (*bāṇas tu gatapattriṇa iti vaijayantī*). Other commentators, who read *śara*, yet another term meaning 'arrow' offer still more elaborate explanations which try to show that there is no redundancy. See Goldman and Sutherland Goldman 2017, 506.

23. Goldman and Sutherland Goldman 2017, 78–81 and Brockington, 1998, 392.
24. It is interesting to note that the various styles of pārāyaṇa all begin with its highly treasured Sundarakāṇḍa and then proceed through the sixth and seventh books before returning to the opening Bālakāṇḍa and reading through to the epic's end. On this see Goldman and Sutherland Goldman, 1996, 79–86.
25. *VR* 5.13.18–24,27–37.
26. *VR* 5.4.1–6.
27. *VR* 6.46.25–28.
28. *VR* 7.31.20–23.
29. *VR* 6.5.4–8.
30. For a detailed discussion of this seminal passage and its treatment by Abhinavagupta, see Masson 1969.

Abbreviations

DhvĀlo	*Dhvanyāloka* of Ānandavardhana (Tripathi 1963)
Loc	*Locana* of Abhinavagupta (Tripathi 1963)
Mbh	*Mahābhārata*, BORI critical edition (Sukthankar, et al. 1933–1970)
MbhC	*Mahābhārata*, Chitrashala Press edition (1929)
UttaRāC	*Uttararāmacarita* (Belvalkar 1922)
VR	*Vālmīki Rāmāyaṇa*, OIB critical edition (Bhatt and Shah 1960–1975)

Works Cited

Arnold, Matthew. 1896. *On Translating Homer.* London: Smith, Elder & Co.

Auerbach, Erich. 2003. *Mimesis: The Representation of Reality in Western Literature.* Translated from the German by Willard R. Trask. With a new introduction by Edward W. Said. Princeton, N.J.: Princeton University Press.

Bandhu, Vishva, ed. 1928–1947. *Rāmāyana.* 7 vols. Lahore: D.A.V. College. Northwestern recension critically edited for the first time from original manuscripts. D.A.V. College Sanskrit Series, nos. 7, 12, 14, 17–20.

Barthes, Roland. 1968. La mort de l'auteur. *Manteia* 5: 61–67.

Belvalkar, Shripad Krishna, ed. 1922. *Uttararāmacaritam of Bhavabhūti.* Bombay: Nirṇayasāgar Press. Published by arrangement with Harvard UP. Originally, *Rama's Later History, or Uttara-Rama-Charita. Part 2: The Text, with Indexes, Glossaries, etc.* Harvard Oriental Series, vol. 22.

Bhatt, G.H. and U.P. Shah, eds. 1960–1975. *Vālmīki Rāmāyaṇa: Critical Edition.* 7 vols. Baroda: Oriental Institute.

Brockington, John. 1998. *The Sanskrit Epics.* Leiden: E. J. Brill.

Bryant, William Cullen, tr. 1898. *The Iliad of Homer: Translated into English Blank Verse.* Boston: Houghton, Mifflin and Company.

Butler, Samuel, tr. 1952. *The Iliad of Homer rendered into English Prose.* Chicago: Encyclopædia Britannica.

Carey, William, and Joshua Marshman, trs. 1806–1810. *The Ramayuna of Valmeeki, in the Original Sungskrit. With a Prose Translation, and Explanatory Notes.* 3 vols. Serampore: N.p.

Chitrashala Press. 1929. *Mahābhārata.* 6 vols. With the commentary of Nīlakaṇṭha. Poona: Chitrashala Press.

Debroy, Bibek. 2017. *The Valmiki Ramayana.* Penguin Books.

Fitzgerald, Robert, tr. 1974. *The Iliad by Homer.* Garden City, NY: Anchor Press.

Gita Press. *Śrīmad Vālmīki-Rāmāyaṇa.* 1969. 3 vols. Tr. Chimmanlal Goswami. Gorakhpur: Gita Press.

Gita Press. *Śrīmad Vālmīki-Rāmāyaṇa.* 1998. 2 vols. 5th ed. Gorakhpur: Gita Press.

Goldman, Robert P. 2018. *Kāvyamaya Itihāsa* and *Aitihāsika Kāvya* Revisited: Vision, Facticity and Historical Consciousness in the Sanskrit Epics and their Commentaries. In *Questioning Paradigms, Constructing Histories: A Festschrift for Romila Thapar.* Eds. Kumkum Roy and Naina Dayal. New Delhi: Aleph Book Company. 159–74.

———. 2020.

———. 2021. *Ā Garbhāt*: Murderous Rage and Collective Punishment as Thematic Elements in Vyāsa's *Mahābhārata.* In *Many Mahābhāratas,* ed. Nell Shapiro Hawley and Sohini Sarah Pillai. Albany: SUNY Press, 37–52.

Goldman, Robert P., et al, eds and trs. 1984–2017. *The Rāmāyaṇa of Vālmīki: An Epic of Ancient India.* 7 vols. Princeton, N.J.: Princeton University Press.

Goldman, Robert P., and Sally J. Sutherland Goldman, eds. and trs. 1996. *The Rāmāyaṇa of Vālmīki: An Epic of Ancient India.* Vol. 5: *Sundarakāṇḍa.* Introduction by Robert P. Goldman and Sally J. Sutherland Goldman. Princeton, N.J.: Princeton Princeton University Press.

———, eds. and trs. 2017. *The Rāmāyaṇa of Vālmīki: An Epic of Ancient India.* Vol. 7: *Uttarakāṇḍa.* Introduction by Robert P. Goldman and Sally J. Sutherland Goldman. Princeton, N.J.: Princeton University Press.

Goldman, Robert P., Sally J. Sutherland Goldman, and Barend A. van Nooten, trs. 2009. *The Rāmāyaṇa of Vālmīki: An Epic of Ancient India.* Vol. 6: *Yuddhakāṇḍa.* Edited with introduction by Robert P. Goldman and Sally J. Sutherland Goldman. Princeton, N.J.: Princeton University Press.

Goldman, Robert P. Vālmīki's Children: Adulation, Imitation and Ethical Critique in Poets of the Rāmakathā. In *Rivista Degli Studi Orientali,* Nuova Serie. Volume XCII, Fasc. 1–2, 2019. pp. 93–103

Gorresio, Gaspare, ed. 1843–1867. *Ramayana, poema indiano di Valmici.* Paris: Stamperia Reale.

Krishnacharya, T.R., and T.R. Vyasacharya, eds. 1911–1913. *Śrīmadvālmīkirāmāyaṇam.* 7 vols. Bombay: Nirnayasagar Press. Also called the Kumbakonam Edition. Reprint 1930.

Lord, Albert Bates. 1960. *The Singer of Tales*. Cambridge, MA: Harvard UP.

Masson, J.L. 1969. 'Who Killed Cock Krauñca? Abhinavagupta's Reflections on the Origin of Aesthetic Experience.' *Journal of the Oriental Institute Baroda* 19: 207–24.

Mudholkar, Shastri Shrinivas Katti, ed. 1914–1920. *Ramayan of Valmiki*. 7 vols. Bombay: Gujarati Printing Press. With three commentaries called Tilaka, Shiromani, and Bhooshana.

Parab, Kāśināth Pāṇḍuraṅg, ed. 1888. *The Rāmāyaṇa of Vālmīki*. Bombay: Nirṇayasāgar Press. With the commentary (*Tilaka*) of Rāma.

Pike, Kenneth L. 1967. Language in Relations to a Unified Theory of Human Behavior (Second Revised ed.). The Hague: Mouton & Co., 37–72.

Pollock, Sheldon. 2016. *A Rasa Reader: Classical Indian Aesthetics*. New York: Columbia University Press.

Ramanujan, A.K. 1991.'Three Hundred Ramayanas: Five Examples and Three Thoughts on Translation'. In *Many Rāmāyaṇas: The Diversity of a Narrative Tradition in South Asia.* Ed. Paula Richman. Berkeley: University of California Press, 22–49.

Schwab, Raymond. 1984. *The Oriental Renaissance: Europe's Rediscovery of India and the East, 1680–1880 (Social Foundations of Aesthetic Forms).* New York: Columbia University Press.

Shastri, Hari Prasad, tr. 1952–1959. *The Ramayana of Valmiki*. 3 vols. London: Shanti Sadan. Rev. 2nd ed. in 2 vols. 1962–1970.

Śrīkṛṣṇadāsa, Gaṅgāviṣṇu, ed. 1935. *Śrīmadvālmīkirāmāyaṇam*. 3 vols. Bombay: Lakṣmīveṅkateśvara Mudranālaya. With the commentaries of Govindarāja, Rāmānuja, and Maheśvaratīrtha and the commentary known as Taniśloki.

Sukthankar, V. S., et al, eds.1933–1970. *The Mahābhārata: For the First Time Critically Edited.* 24 vols. Poona: Bhandarkar Oriental Research Institute.

Tripathi, Ram Sagar, ed.1963. *Dhvanyāloka of Shri Anandavardhanacharya with the Lochan Commentary by Shri Abhinava Gupta along with Full Hindi Translation of Both the Texts and Tarawati Vyakhya*. Delhi: Motilal Banarsidass.